FUNCTIONAL BEHAVIORAL ASSESSMENT

D1559839

OXFORD WORKSHOP SERIES:

SCHOOL SOCIAL WORK ASSOCIATION OF AMERICA

Series Advisory Board

Rochelle Leiber-Miller, President
Frederick Streeck, Executive Director
Michelle E. Alvarez
Vaughn Morrison
Christine Plackis

Evidence-Based Practice in School Mental Health
James C. Raines

The Domains and Demands of School Social Work Practice:
A Guide to Working Effectively with Students, Families, and Schools
Michael S. Kelly

Solution-Focused Brief Therapy in Schools:
A 360-Degree View of Research and Practice
Michael S. Kelly, Johnny S. Kim, and Cynthia Franklin

A New Model of School Discipline:
Engaging Students and Preventing Behavior Problems
David R. Dupper

Truancy Prevention and Intervention:
A Practical Guide
Lynn Bye, Michelle E. Alvarez, Janet Haynes, and Cindy E. Sweigart

Ethical Decision Making in School Mental Health
James C. Raines and Nic T. Dibble

Functional Behavioral Assessment:
A Three-Tiered Prevention Model
Kevin J. Filter and Michelle E. Alvarez

FUNCTIONAL BEHAVIORAL ASSESSMENT

A Three-Tiered Prevention Model

Kevin J. Filter
Michelle E. Alvarez

OXFORD WORKSHOP SERIES

OXFORD
UNIVERSITY PRESS

Published in the United States of America by Oxford University Press, Inc.,
198 Madison Avenue, New York, NY, 10016
United States of America

Oxford University Press, Inc., publishes works that further Oxford University's
objective of excellence in research, scholarship, and education

Library of Congress Cataloging-in-Publication Data

Filter, Kevin J.
Functional behavioral assessment : a three-tiered prevention
model / Kevin J. Filter, Michelle E. Alvarez.
p. cm. — (Oxford workshop series)
Includes bibliographical references and index.
ISBN 978-0-19-976493-8 (pbk. : alk. paper)
1. Behavior modification—Methodology. 2. Behavioral assessment—Methodology.
3. Problem children—Education. I. Alvarez, Michelle. II. Title.
LB1060.2.F55 2011
370.15'28—dc23   2011027002

1 3 5 7 9 10 8 6 4 2

Typeset in Berkeley Font
Printed on acid-free paper
Printed in United States

Acknowledgments

I would like to acknowledge Dr. Rob Horner and Dr. George Sugai for their efforts in improving schools through Positive Behavior Interventions and Supports (PBIS) and for their support in the writing of this book. I would also like to acknowledge the leadership of the Minnesota PBIS Initiative for the opportunities that they have given me to work with schools implementing three-tiered functional models of behavior support. Above all, my wife Susan Filter and my children have been very supportive, and this book would not have been possible without their patience and love. Finally, I would like to acknowledge my co-author, Michelle, for all of her tireless work, and Rachel Youngblom and Jules Nolan for the work they put into reviewing drafts of this book and organizing references.

Kevin J. Filter

I would like to acknowledge my co-author, Dr. Kevin Filter, who brings years of experience and professional wisdom to the book. He has put long hours into the content of the book, and I want him to know it is appreciated. I would also like to acknowledge my husband Marvin, and children Kipp, Karolina, and Kristian for their support of my projects. All of this work could not have been done without my school social work experience in Pinellas County Public Schools (Florida), Marion County Schools (Florida), Evansville-Vanderburgh School Corporation, and the insight and support from school social workers and students from across the United States that have allowed me to share their experiences. Finally, thank you to Maura Roessner and Nicholas Liu from Oxford University Press for their continued support.

Michelle E. Alvarez

Contents

FUNCTIONAL BEHAVIORAL ASSESSMENT

I

Functional Behavioral Assessment and School Social Work

In this chapter, a brief history of functional behavioral assessment (FBA) is explored, the relevance of FBA to school social work is addressed, a review is made of those skills that school social workers already possess and that can contribute to the FBA process, and potential roles for school social workers in the FBA process are outlined. The chapter concludes with a summary of the themes that provide a foundation for this book.

The importance of a link between FBA and school social work practice cannot be overemphasized. Clark and Thiede (2007) stated that school social work assessment in special education was no longer centered on the study of students' social developmental histories. Clark and Alvarez (2010) affirmed this observation that FBA and the resulting behavioral intervention plan (BIP) would replace the social developmental history as the primary assessment tool that school social workers utilize in practice. Clark, Alvarez, Marckmann, and Timm (2010) noted that, in order to play a significant role in a Response to Intervention (RtI) framework,

> School social workers will need to be proficient in conducting functional behavior assessments. This approach to assessment facilitates an understanding of the function or purpose of behavior and provides data that are useful in designing interventions. A functional approach to assessment also helps maintain a constant focus on problem solving and ensuring positive educational results, and it diminishes the need for labeling and categorizing students. (pp. 258–259)

Use of the FBA process goes beyond the value of actively participating in the school's efforts to implement an RtI framework; it is a research-based practice that improves student outcomes (Kern, Gallagher, Starosta, Hickman, & George, 2006).

Definition and History of Functional Behavioral Assessment

FBA is a process for identifying the environmental conditions that predict and maintain problem behavior (O'Neill et al., 1997). The identification of environmental conditions relevant to behavior can be accomplished in many different ways, including direct observation, interviews, and record reviews, and one of the primary purposes of this book is to highlight the range of procedures that can be utilized in this process. FBA has become important to school-based practice because it directly informs successful interventions. Therefore, a proper FBA can be considered complete when it has been translated into an effective intervention.

To understand why FBA is relevant to school social work practice, it is important to know a brief history of its development and its later use in schools. Although early research in this area was with animals and not humans, it laid the foundation for identifying the function of behavior. Thorndike (1913) identified the *Law of Effect*: behaviors that obtain desired outcomes tend to recur. He followed Pavlov and influenced Watson (1924), both of whom focused on the behavior elicited from stimuli—the notion that behavior is a reflexive reaction to antecedent events in the environment. Skinner (1938) found that behavior was a function of environmental conditions and was reinforced by the consequences that followed it. Skinner's work emphasized that the environment affects voluntary behavior (i.e., we choose to engage in behavior that works) as well as involuntary, reflexive behavior. Skinner (1953) first used the term *functional analysis* to refer to a systematic method of exploring the interactions between a problem behavior and the environment. Skinner's empirical and theoretical work in behavioral science laid the foundation for later research by others in the area of behavioral interventions. During the late 1950s and 1960s, behavioral intervention research was published focusing on the use of reinforcement and punishment to override existing contingent relationships between behavior and environment, but this approach did not base interventions on the assessment of functional relations. Bijou, Peterson, and Ault (1968) were the first researchers to study the identification of the purpose of existing behavior (function), utilizing the antecedent-behavior-consequence (ABC) method of recording behavior. Carr (1977) conducted a meta-analysis hypothesizing that problem behaviors recur due to either positive reinforcement, negative reinforcement, sensory stimulation, or a biological disorder. The meta-analysis found that these four hypothesized reasons for the recurrence of behavior were statistically significant. The concept was furthered when Iwata, Dorsey, Slifer, Bauman, and Richman (1982) developed the methodology with which to conduct an experimental functional analysis to identify the purpose (function) of behavior by controlling antecedents and consequences and measuring their effects on behavior.

During the 1990s, research focused on the idea that although two students were exhibiting similar behaviors, the function of their behaviors could be different (Mace & Roberts, 1993). This research emphasized the need to properly identify the individualized function of the behavior, without assuming that similar behavior indicates similar function. More emphasis was then placed on systematic methods of identifying the function of behavior, using experimental research studies designed to determine the function of behavior. Iwata et al. (1982) developed the first comprehensive functional analysis of self-injurious behavior by studying the positive, negative, and automatic reinforcements of this type of behavior. This was accomplished by systematically controlling antecedents and consequences in a number of experimental conditions to determine which conditions led to the most problem behaviors. Up to this point in the history of FBA, procedures had been limited to controlled experimental environments (e.g., clinic labs).

It was not until recently that research on FBA moved into a less controlled environment—the public education setting. In making this move to less controlled environments, new methods for conducting FBAs were explored, ones that relied more on indirect data sources (e.g., interviews, archival records) and nonexperimental direct data sources (e.g., systematic direct observation). Although the focus was originally on the use of FBA in special education, more recent studies have demonstrated its effectiveness in general education. Researchers began to train general education teachers to conduct FBAs; they evaluated the fidelity with which they were implemented (Lane, Weisenbach, Little, Phillips, & Wehby, 2006; Maag & Larson, 2004) and found that, with support, teachers were able to conduct and implement interventions associated with FBAs. Patterson's work (2009) and similar studies researched the fidelity with which teachers implemented an FBA without the support of a university researcher. Patterson (2009) found that, despite some limitations, general education teachers could design and implement FBAs. However, the research did note some barriers to implementation by teachers, including professional development, administrative support, comfort level with data collection, and incorporation of the process into the school day (Patterson, 2009).

Research prompted a shift to focusing on the replacement of unwanted behaviors with more appropriate behaviors using positive interventions rather than negative consequences.

In summary, FBA is based on more than half a century of experimental research demonstrating the relationship between environment and behavior, the purposefulness of problem behavior to meet basic human needs, principles of learning and instruction, and the ability of environmental redesign to make problem behaviors irrelevant, inefficient, and ineffective (McIntosh, Brown, & Borgmeier, 2008, p. 7).

A historical review of FBAs demonstrates the evolution of a research-based practice and its eventual applicability and practicality in a general education setting. In this book, we further this historical trend by describing how FBA can be applied to all three tiers of a prevention model, in order to help all students in a school, including those with and without severe problem behavior.

Current Research-based Support

Although more detailed research is addressed in Chapter 2, it is important to stress that, in this book, we present information about the use of FBA in general education because of its proven effectiveness in addressing the continuum of student behavioral challenges, from their first appearance to their long-term presence. A demonstrated precision in identifying the function of a behavior was found with the use of an ABC process (Hanley, Iwata, & McCord, 2003), the effectiveness of FBAs has been demonstrated (Ingram, Lewis-Palmer, & Sugai, 2005), and the longevity of the outcomes from implementing a behavior plan based on FBA has been supported (Kern et al., 2006). When the function of a behavior is identified, there is a documented increase in the effectiveness of the intervention (Filter & Horner, 2009; Ingram et al., 2005; Newcomer & Lewis, 2004). Finally, the overall effectiveness of the process has been established (Ingram et al., 2005), and its consistency with school social work practice has been noted (Tracy & Usaj, 2007).

When FBAs are conducted in a systematic manner, the function of a behavior is precisely identified, interventions specific to the identified function of a behavior are implemented, and response to the intervention is tracked; the process mimics a single-subject research design methodology. Horner, Carr, Halle, McGee, Odom, and Wolery (2005) note that, "single subject design is a rigorous, scientific methodology used to define basic principles of behavior and establish evidence-based practices" (p. 165). Use of FBAs in general education is a research-based method to address target behaviors and can be applied to all tiers in an RtI framework.

Relevance to School Social Work

There is a lack of school social work literature related to FBA, as evidenced by a limited number of articles or book chapters that address the use of FBAs in school social work practice. This lack of scholarly resources on FBA in school social work practice is surprising because school social workers have been conducting FBAs in special education since their inclusion in the Individuals with Disabilities Education Action of 1997 (IDEA) (P.L. 105–17) and its reauthorization in 2004. The use of FBA with special education students (Tracy & Usaj, 2007), its consistency with school social work practice (Tracy & Usaj, 2007), and its fit with an ecological approach (Clark & Thiede, 2007; Tracy & Usaj, 2007) and strengths-based practice (Clark & Thiede, 2007) have been addressed.

Only recently have FBAs become an assessment tool utilized in general education. Clark and Alvarez (2010) advocate for the use of FBAs as a primary assessment tool for school social workers, supplemented only when necessary by the more traditional social developmental history.

Skills

Harrison and Harrison (2009) identified those existing school social work skills that contribute to the implementation of a systematic FBA process. Although mentioned specifically in relation to the tertiary level of prevention, these same skills can be applied at all tiers of an RtI framework. These skills included facilitating the composition of functional assessment teams that include family members, the analysis of human behavior, the communication between multidisciplinary stakeholders, the gathering of multilayered information, the identification of student strengths, the development of comprehensive interventions, and the measurement of outcomes.

Role

School social workers are keenly aware of the resources available within the community. Often called the *vital link*, school social workers link the school with the family and community, and this can contribute to the academic success of students (Jozefowicz-Simbeni, 2008; Shaffer, 2007). Many schools are

---

located in communities possessing untapped resources of which schools may not be aware (Anderson-Butcher, Stetler, & Midle, 2006). By leveraging these resources, the school and community work together to address those barriers to learning identified in an FBA. Recognizing the value of working as a liaison, Anderson-Butcher, Stetler, and Midle (2006) state that social workers are key players who promote coordination; connect programs, services, and other resources; provide leadership in community mobilization efforts; and advocate for those in need of additional supports and resources. Therefore, one of the unique roles that school social workers bring to the FBA process is their ability to tap into existing resources to address issues.

Leadership is another role that school social workers can bring to the process (Clark & Gilmore, 2010). Because of the nature of their work with students, school social workers are often aware of internal and external stakeholders, including school personnel who are not obvious candidates for the team (such as bus drivers and janitors) and community agencies that already provide services to particular students; these participants can play an integral role on the team (Harrison & Harrison, 2009).

With their substantial training and knowledge in systems theory, school social workers can promote team-based decision-making through purposeful communication across home, school, and community (Fynaardt & Richardson, 2010; Harrison & Harrison, 2009). As the team selects methods for data collection, school social workers can call upon their experience in gathering information from multiple sources within the school, family, and community, and synthesizing the information to present to the team and family (Fynaardt & Richardson, 2010; Clark & Gilmore, 2010; Harrison & Harrison, 2009). School social workers also have well-developed interviewing skills that include active listening, use of reflective statements, and reframing, which can be utilized across settings.

School social workers are trained in strengths-based approaches to replace undesired behaviors, and these approaches play a significant role in the development of positive behavior intervention plans (Fynaardt & Richardson, 2010; Harrison & Harrison, 2009). Last, school social workers abide by the National Association of Social Workers Code of Ethics (2008), prompting them as team members to ensure ethical decision-making related to collecting and reporting information in a respectful manner that preserves the dignity of the student (Harrison & Harrison, 2009).

A collaborating role for school social workers is that of liaison with the family. The family is directly impacted by the student's behavior and can

Functional Behavioral Assessment

provide a wealth of information about attempts to address the behavior. School social workers can involve the family in the FBA process by inviting family members to be part of the FBA team (Chandler & Dahlquist, 2010; Salend & Taylor, 2002; Scott & Eber, 2003), assigning a role to the family in the school-based BIP (Chandler & Dahlquist, 2010), involving the family in conducting FBAs in the home setting, and developing a BIP (Chandler & Dahlquist, 2010; Cormier, 2009; McNeill, Watson, Henington, & Meeks, 2002) that complements the school-based teams plan.

Developing and Maintaining Skills

The process of conducting an FBA at any tier requires the work of a team to ensure process fidelity and to conduct ongoing evaluation of the process. Although Chapter 2 will review the definitions and underlying concepts of an evidence-based FBA process, the case example in Box 1.1 demonstrates the importance of ongoing professional development in developing, maintaining, and improving practice.

Box 1.1 A Model for Professional Development

In 2005, Heartland Area Education Agency 11 in Johnston, Iowa, initiated a case review process to provide continuous practice feedback to school social workers implementing RtI systems. Heartland AEA is located in the central area of Iowa; it serves 54 public school districts and 32 nonpublic schools. It employed 44 school social workers at the time this professional development activity commenced.

The purpose of the school social work case review process was to improve the proficiency of school social workers in implementing problem-solving practices with individual students. Case reviews provided an opportunity for work with individual students to be shared with a small group of peers. The process involved reflection and discussion of how decisions were made based on data, evaluation of the problem-solving process, and implications of assessments and decisions. The intent was to create a supportive environment in which the focus was on improving practice. Group sessions were

---

held regionally with four to eight school social workers participating in each group.

In the third year, case reviews focused on the components of FBA and intervention. The agency had initiated the use of new FBA forms and had an increased expectation for documentation. FBA and behavior intervention plan rubrics were developed for use in evaluating practice. Components that were focused on during peer case reviews included definition of problem behavior, indirect analysis, direct analysis, hypothesis of function of behavior, and definition of replacement behavior. The intervention components that were focused on included strategy for teaching replacement behavior, procedures for display of problematic behavior, outline of supports to assist teacher implementation, data collection procedures, and degree to which the data-based decision-making rubric was utilized. Each group reviewed documentation and agreed upon a rating for each component. The group rating was recorded and averaged to determine group performance. The results of case reviews led the school social workers to identify specific areas for further development. The Heartland AEA school social workers found the case review process to be an effective method for providing continuous professional development.

Adapted from Clark, J. P., Alvarez, M. E., Marckmann, W., & Tim, A. (2010). Supporting the adoption, implementation, and sustainability of RtI systems. In J. P. Clark & M. E. Alvarez (Eds.), *Response to intervention: A guide for school social workers*. New York: Oxford University Press.

Summary

The authors have integrated the following themes in this book:

- A contextual/environmental perspective on student behavior
- FBAs as relevant to all students
- FBA as a general education process with relevance to special education
- A three-tiered prevention model around which the chapters are organized

- The preservation of assessment information across all tiers of prevention
- FBA as a team-managed process.

It is clear that school social workers have unique skills to contribute to the FBA process. The purpose of this book is to prompt thinking about how this research-based process for addressing behavior in school can be implemented in general education to produce successful outcomes for students. We also hope to increase the awareness of school social workers that FBAs can be used at all tiers of prevention. This book is organized around the tiers of prevention, in recognition of the fact that components of the FBA process can be effectively utilized across all three tiers (see Figure 1.1). Although the rigor and intensity of an FBA at Tier 1 will differ from the rigor and intensity at Tier 3, thinking functionally about behavior can facilitate good outcomes for students. Consistent with a three-tiered prevention model, FBAs are relevant to *all* students, especially those being served in the general education setting. Although FBAs were first used with students with disabilities, the contextual understanding of behavior has significant implications for improving the behavior of students without disabilities. Finally, the process of collecting data and planning interventions in an FBA model is managed by a team

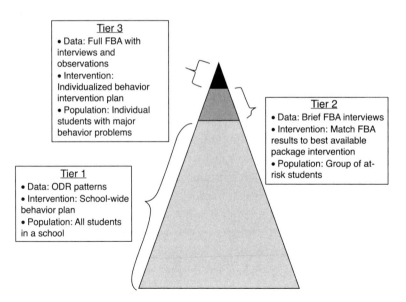

FIGURE 1.1 Functional behavioral assessment across three tiers of prevention.

rather than by an individual. This ensures input from multiple sources and shared responsibility for outcomes.

School social workers have most likely been introduced to the three-tiered model of prevention or the RtI framework for the delivery of services to students. Tiers are often presented in a triangular figure, with the base representing Tier 1 or universal/school-wide services provided to all students; the center level represents Tier 2 services or targeted group interventions, and the tip of the triangle represents Tier 3 or intensive individual services. In the literature, the broad concept of RtI is defined by Batsche et al. (2005) as, "The practice of providing high-quality instruction and interventions matched to student need, monitoring progress frequently to make decisions about changes in instruction or goals, and applying child response data to important educational decisions" (p. 3). Clark and Alvarez (2010) define it as, "A multitiered framework for organizing evidenced-based practices in a systematic process for the purpose of determining what interventions ensure the academic, social, emotional, and behavioral success of all students" (p. xiv). These definitions highlight themes such as high-quality interventions, data-based decision making, and progress monitoring—all of which are enhanced by the use of FBAs when dealing with behavioral problems.

We believe that school FBAs must target alterable, educationally relevant behaviors. The contextual/environmental perspective must be maintained. School social workers are asked to address many issues that go beyond that of the behavior exhibited in school. However, social work practices in schools require a focus on education and those issues that interfere with the school's ability to provide the student with an education. Therefore, behaviors targeted by school-based FBAs occur in the school setting and may or may not occur in the home or community setting. Also consistent with RtI, it is important to preserve assessment information throughout the process of working at all tiers. FBAs at previous tiers will inform work at the other tiers, if that becomes necessary. Information gathered at Tier 1 regarding all students can inform more individualized FBAs conducted at Tier 2 or 3 and vice versa.

Finally, this book was written to provide school social workers with the practical tools they need to implement FBAs across all tiers. Possible case examples and sample forms are provided to assist in this process. The application of FBA across tiers, especially at Tiers 1 and 2, is a new concept, and this book attempts to synthesize the current knowledge base in this area and recommend practices that lead to positive outcomes for all students, including those with or without severe problem behaviors.

2

■■■

The Importance and Foundation of Functional Behavioral Assessment in a Three-Tiered Model

The suggestion that schools generally need to improve their management of student behavior is a well-accepted truth. It is clear from data on office discipline referrals that the level of problem behavior in schools is substantial and that teachers clearly consider student behavior problems to have an adverse affect on them and on students (Skiba, Peterson, & Williams, 1997; Spaulding et al., 2010; Westling, 2010). Therefore, the search for effective ways of improving student behavior has been a major endeavor, and several methods of reducing problem behavior have emerged, each with varying degrees of success. One method is punishment, which involves waiting until problem behavior occurs and then providing aversive consequences in the hopes that the behavior will be less likely to occur in the future. Although punishment can be effective in limited circumstances, it is associated with a number of predictable side effects, such as emotional responding, avoidance of the people who deliver punishment, and continued covert problem behavior (Miltenberger, 2004). Further, when punishment-oriented methods of behavior management have been applied in large-scale efforts—as is the case with "zero tolerance" policies in schools—no clear evidence of improvements in behavior has emerged (Skiba & Peterson, 1999). A second, more promising and positive method of reducing problem behavior is to focus on preventing problems and teaching and reinforcing more appropriate behavior. A brief review of the literature supporting these methods will be offered later in this chapter, but it suffices for now to say that there has been a significant amount of research supporting this positive approach to behavior management and that the development of these positive interventions is dependent on the gathering of information from a functional behavioral assessment (FBA). As can be seen in Table 2.1, an FBA will tell us the antecedents to the problem behavior, thereby informing the prevention of the behavior; the problem behavior itself, thereby informing the selection of alternative behaviors to teach; and the main consequences of the problem behavior, thereby informing those consequences that can be used to reinforce more appropriate behavior. It is import to note that FBAs not only allow us to develop interventions using positive strategies, but also that school-based interventions based on FBAs lead to more successful reductions in problem behavior than do school-based interventions that are not based on FBAs (Filter & Horner, 2009; Ingram, Lewis-Palmer, & Sugai, 2005; Newcomer & Lewis, 2004).

Table 2.1 Examples of how the information from an FBA can inform positive behavior change strategies

Information from an FBA	Informs the Following Interventions	For Example:
Setting events* (Events that set up the problem behavior)	Setting event manipulations	If a student's behavior is precipitated by a lack of sleep, then the social worker can help the family change the student's sleep schedule.
Antecedents* (Events that set off the problem behavior)	Antecedent manipulations	If a student's behavior is triggered by difficult tasks, then the task can be modified to match the student's skill level.
Problem behavior*	Behavior manipulations (behavioral teaching)	If a student is swearing, and the swearing is maintained by peer attention, then she could be taught a more appropriate way and time to get peer attention (e.g., talking about video games during lunch).
Consequence* (The reinforcers that maintain the behavior)	Consequence manipulations	Appropriate behaviors could be reinforced using the same consequence that maintained the problem behavior.

*For technical definitions of these terms, see the section of this chapter labeled, *Basic Concepts in the Functional Model of Behavior* on p. 22.

Furthermore, even when working with many students at the Tier 1 level of prevention, evidence suggests that student behavior improves significantly when antecedents, behaviors, and consequences are analyzed and data are applied during intervention (Hirsch, Lewis-Palmer, Sugai, & Schnacker, 2004; Luiselli, Putnam, & Sunderland, 2002).

Legal Foundations

It should be clear by now that FBAs can make an important contribution to the improvement of student behavior in schools. In addition to the empirical support for FBAs, there is also a clear legal foundation for the use of FBAs in schools. In 1997, the reauthorization of the Individuals with Disabilities Education Act (IDEA) included specific language relating to the use of FBAs. This was the first federal mandate for FBAs in schools. The most recent reauthorization of the legislation, IDEA 2004, maintains most of the provisions of the 1997 version and will be reviewed here for its relevance to FBAs. It is important to note that the legal requirements for FBAs conform to the process that will be described in this book as a Tier 3 FBA, which targets individual students with significant and/or dangerous problem behaviors. There is no clear legal requirement for FBA at tiers 1 and 2 of a prevention model. However, education laws represents the minimal criterion for when and how certain professional services should be offered in the schools, and the lack of legal mandates for Tier 1 and Tier 2 FBAs should not be taken as reasons not to conduct them. The true value of FBA at any tier is its contribution to positive student outcomes, more so than its function as a legal requirement.

IDEA 2004 specifies that individual (Tier 3) FBAs must be conducted for students who have been identified with a disability, when they have been removed from school for more than 10 cumulative days, or when the student's behavior is considered to significantly interfere with the learning environment. In regards to the criterion of 10 cumulative days of removal, IDEA specifies that this criterion is to be understood as relevant only when the 10 days of removal constitute a clear pattern. So, short removals for a number of different incidents throughout a year would not necessarily constitute a clear pattern, and probably would not require an FBA to be completed (von Ravensberg & Tobin, 2006). However, the conservative interpretation of the law would be to conduct an FBA for any cumulative 10 days of removal. The 10-day removal process also triggers the process of a *manifestation determination*, which is a process whereby the team managing the Individual Education Program (IEP) for a particular student with a disability determines whether the problem behavior was a result of the disability or not. Therefore, FBA requirements are also tied to manifestation determinations for students with disabilities, such that an FBA must be conducted regardless of the results of the manifestation determination in order to develop a positive behavior intervention plan (van Ravensberg & Tobin).

The guidelines for the requirement to conduct an FBA whenever behavior significantly interferes with the learning environment are less clear. However, when it is clear that the behavior of a student with a disability is interfering with his or her ability to learn, the IEP team should review the student's records to determine if an FBA that could be used in developing a better positive behavior intervention plan (BIP) has been conducted recently. The team should conduct an FBA if none has recently occurred. Although IDEA legislation is not clear in describing what behavior should fall into this category, Drasgow, Yell, Bradley, and Shriner (1999) suggest that we can infer from previous litigation that the following behaviors should result in an FBA that informs a positive BIP: "(a) disruptive behaviors that distract the teacher from teacher and other students from learning, (b) noncompliance, (c) abuse of property, (d) verbal abuse, and (e) aggression towards students or staff" (p. 245).

It is clear from the law that the purpose of conducting an FBA under these specified circumstances is to develop a positive BIP that will result in a decrease in problem behaviors and increased opportunities for the student to participate in the academic environment. This point has sometimes been overlooked since IDEA was enacted. Schools that have overlooked the interventional purpose of the FBA have created the "file drawer" phenomenon, whereby FBAs are conducted when required but are not used in developing plans that will help students. Readers of this book should be clear that an FBA should automatically trigger the development of a BIP for a student. The process for developing positive BIPs based on the results of an FBA will be covered in depth in Chapter 7.

It is also important to note that three-tiered, FBA-based approaches to dealing with problem behavior seem to be increasing in their legal relevance over time. At the time of writing, the reauthorization of the federal Elementary and Secondary Education Act was being developed and included an increased focus on function-based preventative behavior interventions in schools, in the form of school-wide positive behavior support. It is likely that future legislation and legal rulings will continue to emphasize this approach and that those who are competent in three-tiered FBAs will be valuable assets to their schools.

The Functional Model of Behavior that Underlies Functional Behavioral Assessment

Why do students misbehave? Or, really, why do any students do what they do? The reason we want to know this is that once we know *why* they do what they do, we can use that knowledge to change what they do. So, let's start with some simple examples and consider some possible explanations for the behavior. Let's begin with Brett.

Assumptions of the Functional Model

The functional model of behavior—as illustrated in the below examples of Brett, Natasha, the good student, and the messy teachers—assumes that (a) behavior is purposeful, (b) behavior is learned, and (c) behavior can be changed. These assumptions are well-supported by 40 years of solid research

---

Brett Makes the Teacher Angry

Brett is a fourth-grade student who makes mean comments and jokes about the teacher to other students when her back is turned to him. The teacher hears the other kids laughing and knows that something inappropriate has happened. She confronts the class and asks, "What's going on?"

Why is Brett making mean comments and jokes behind the teacher's back? Let's begin with some easy explanations:

- Brett is a naughty student.
- Brett is a class clown.
- Brett is an uncaring person.

The theme across these explanations is that they are character descriptions—descriptions about Brett and his fundamental nature as a person. These descriptions demonstrate what social psychologists call the *fundamental attribution error* (Ross, 1977), which is a tendency to overestimate the influence of internal factors when

---

explaining the behavior of others. Not only is this a predictable social error, but it also directs us away from those conditions in the environment that could be causing this behavior. Once we know the environmental conditions related to the behavior, we can change those conditions to change the behavior.

Let's consider some alternative explanations for Brett's behavior that may be more helpful:

- Brett is trying to *obtain peer attention*: Perhaps Brett has learned that his peers usually laugh at these comments and jokes, and he likes this kind of attention.
- Brett is trying to *escape an aversive task*: Perhaps Brett knows that he can get out of an assignment by getting the teacher mad and being sent to the office.
- Brett is trying to *obtain a tangible*: Perhaps Brett has worked out bets with one of his peers so that, if he makes these jokes, he will get a set of baseball cards.

The theme across these explanations is that his behavior is maintained by a consequence in his environment. Or, to restate this same idea, there is a *functional* relationship between Brett's behavior and its consequences. Consequences can be manipulated—perhaps not always with ease, but they can be changed. Therefore, these functional explanations move us in the direction of building a logical positive BIP. The important question from this example is, "Which of these explanations for Brett's behavior is correct?" Of course, we don't have enough information to answer that question right now, but FBA is a process that will allow us to answer that question with a high degree of confidence.

Natasha Skips Class

Natasha is a junior in high school, and she skips algebra class once or twice per week. Her grades over the first quarter placed her at risk for an F, even though she often did quality work when in class. When asked to speculate about her absences, her algebra teacher suggested that she is an angry person, doesn't care about her education, and has been a truant for years. Of course, these explanations fall prey to the fundamental attribution error as well, and they don't help us to determine the functional explanations for her absences. Some possible alternative explanations that do consider functional explanations would be:

- She is trying to *escape an aversive task*: Perhaps she doesn't understand algebra and finds anything more enjoyable than sitting through class.
- She is trying to *obtain sensory stimulation*: Perhaps she is using drugs and can only meet her drug dealer during algebra class.
- She is trying to *obtain peer attention*: Perhaps all of her best friends have an open study hall at the time that she has algebra class, and she wants to gather with them at the pizza place down the street.

Once again, what we really want to know is which of these explanations best fits Natasha's situation. In her case, an FBA conducted by a team led by the school social worker indicated that the peer attention hypothesis was the best explanation. To increase her attendance, the social worker was able to set up a plan whereby regular attendance in algebra class was rewarded with monthly movie tickets donated by the local movie theater for her and her friends. Natasha only missed three more algebra classes over the final next 6 months of her junior year. She earned an A in her final quarter after recovering from a D in her first quarter.

Good Behavior and Teacher Behavior

Although our focus in this book will be on problem behavior, it is important to remember that the functional model applies not only to the inappropriate behaviors of students, but also to the appropriate behaviors of students and the behaviors of adults. The functional model of behavior is not developmental, it is general. It explains a predictable relationship between the environment and behavior. For example, when a student in class asks to work as a tutor for her classmates, it is easy to assume that this student is very considerate and very responsible. From the perspective of the functional model, however, the student may be bored with the activity and may be trying to help others understand it, rather than deal with the monotony of the task. In this case, the tutoring behavior is maintained by *escape from an aversive (boring) task*. It could also be the case that this student really likes it when other students look up to her or when the teacher notices how helpful she is. In that case, her behavior is maintained by *obtaining attention*.

Why do teachers leave messes after staff development training sessions at the district office? It is easy to think of the internal attributions we could make. For example, that teachers who leave messes are lazy, or they don't care about others. Functionally, however, it may be the case that the garbage receptacles are poorly labeled, and the schedule for staff training leaves very little time for appropriate transition behavior. Perhaps the messes left by groups of teachers could be maintained by *access to preferred activities/tasks*—with the preferred activity being the next training session. In other words, these teachers want to get to the next training session so quickly that they leave their garbage at the tables and in the surrounding area. In this case, we've explained the behavior of a group of adults using the same functional model that was applied to students with problem behaviors. Since the functional model can be applied to any behavior at any level of development or prevention, it is also true that FBAs can be conducted with any behavior, at any developmental level, at any level of prevention (e.g., Tier 1, Tier 2, or Tier 3).

published in the *Journal of Applied Behavior Analysis* and similar journals. We will explain each of these assumptions briefly.

Behavior Is Purposeful

To say that behavior is purposeful is to say that behavior does not occur at random. If behavior were random, then it would be equally likely for a school teacher to teach a lesson or do a headstand when students are in the room. Of course, we know that teaching a lesson is a far more likely teacher behavior because that is what we generally observe in classrooms. How often have you seen teachers randomly standing on their heads or rubbing their noses on book shelves? How often have you seen students sliding on their backs down the hall between classes? Almost never. If you did observe this student behavior, then the functional model of behavior assumes that this student is getting something out of sliding on her back down the hallway and, to help her, we would need to find out what that something is.

Behavior occurs because it accomplishes something. The purpose of behavior is generally to obtain favorable consequences and/or avoid aversive consequences. Natasha's behavior in the above example allowed her to gain a favorable consequence; namely, she obtained attention from her peers. Using a functional model of behavior, we can assume that Natasha will not continue to skip class if skipping class no longer leads to peer attention because it would then no longer serve its intended purpose.

Behavior Is Learned

Although there are many possible ways to obtain favorable consequences and avoid aversive consequences, each child has learned to accomplish these goals in very different ways. For example, most children do not like to be yelled at by their parents, so they are generally motivated to avoid it. One child may have learned that she can take a cookie (which is obtaining a favorable consequence) and avoid getting in trouble by lying about taking the cookie. A different child, however, may have learned that his attempts to lie about taking a cookie did not allow him to escape being yelled at. So, the second child would be less likely than the first child to engage in lying as a way to avoid being yelled at. We now have two children who continue to be motivated to avoid being yelled at by parents, but only one who is likely to lie for that reason. One has learned that lying works, and the other has learned that lying doesn't work.

It is easy to see how problem behaviors are the result of learning, but we need to keep in mind that good behavior and problem behaviors are different only in terms of our evaluation of them, not in their nature. Therefore, good behavior is also learned, and more to the point, good behavior can be taught. So, when we expect students to improve their behaviors, we need to keep in mind that adults have a responsibility to create the opportunities for students to learn the good behaviors that we expect.

Behavior Can Be Changed

By understanding that behavior is purposeful—by which we mean it is maintained by consequences—and by understanding that behavior is learned, we can reasonably assume that changing consequences and creating opportunities for students to learn new behaviors can lead to changes in current behavior. Changing current behavior is the ultimate goal of conducting FBAs. FBAs give us the information that allows us to change the environmental conditions so that undesired behavior is no longer necessary. We can also use FBAs to design interventions that will teach students more appropriate ways to obtain the consequences that they are motivated to obtain. The process of developing interventions will be addressed at each tier throughout this book, and a detailed process for using FBAs to build BIPs will be covered in Chapter 7.

Basic Concepts in the Functional Model of Behavior

To this point in the book, we have generally described the fact that FBA is a process of identifying the factors in those environment that control problem behavior so that we can change the behavior. Now, we will describe some of the terminology used in FBAs and lay out the relationship between behavior and the environment in a clear manner.

The foundation of a functional model of behavior is the three-term contingency, including *antecedents*, *behaviors*, and *consequences* (Figure 2.1). *Setting events* have also been added to this model, and their relationship to the three-term contingency will be explained later in the chapter.

Antecedents

Antecedents are the environmental stimuli or events that occur before a behavior and that trigger the behavior. An antecedent is essentially the same concept as *discriminative stimulus*, which is a more technical term used in applied behavior analysis (Cooper, Heron, & Heward, 2007). Discriminative stimulus implies that the controlling power of the antecedent stimulus is its ability to signal the availability of a particular consequence. For example, when a student is engaging in problem behavior in order to obtain teacher

Antecedent ➡ Behavior ➡ Consequence

FIGURE 2.1 The traditional three-term contingency of the functional model of behavior.

attention, the simple presence of that teacher will signal the availability of that consequence and then increase the chance that the problem behavior will occur. Therefore, the discriminative stimulus and the antecedent is the presence of the teacher. However, it is sometimes the case in practice that an adult can recognize that some event typically precedes the occurrence of the problem behavior, even though it is unclear how this event signals the availability of a consequence. In these cases, it is still perfectly acceptable to describe the event as an antecedent for the problem behavior and part of the three-term contingency. By simply knowing that an event or a stimulus typically precedes a problem behavior, we can develop interventions that will change that stimulus or event and thereby change the problem behavior. So, in the most basic sense, an antecedent is simply any stimulus or event that typically precedes the problem behavior.

Behaviors

A behavior is any act by a person that is observable. When conducting an FBA, it will be the case that the target behavior is socially unacceptable and therefore needs to be reduced. In other words, we will only be concerned with problem behaviors.

Consequences

Consequences are stimuli or events that come after a behavior and are contingent upon performance of the behavior. Consequences can be of two types, reinforcers and punishers. *Reinforcers* are consequences that are favorable for the person exhibiting the behavior and increase the future rates or likelihood of the behaviors. *Punishers* are consequences that are unfavorable for the person exhibiting the behavior and decrease the future rates or likelihood of the behaviors. Since punishers decrease behavior, they would not be expected to maintain a problem behavior. Therefore, when conducting an FBA, we will be concerned primarily with reinforcers, because they are the consequences that maintain the problem behavior.

There are two different types of reinforcers, positive reinforcers and negative reinforcers. *Positive reinforcers* are reinforcers that are added to the situation. For example, when a student yells in class and then receives attention from the teacher, the attention from the teacher was something that was not present before the behavior, and it was therefore added to the situation as a result of the behavior. *Negative reinforcers* are stimuli or events that are removed from a situation when a behavior occurs that leads to an increase in the behavior that preceded them. For example, when a student gets out of his seat during independent seatwork that he does not like and then is sent to the office, being sent to the office functions as a negative reinforcer for the behavior because it involves the temporary removal of the independent seatwork demands. In other words, getting out of the seat will be more likely in similar situations in the future because getting out of the seat led to the consequence of escaping the aversive task—an outcome that the child experiences as favorable.

Negative reinforcers and the general phenomenon of negative reinforcement are commonly misunderstood. Negative reinforcement is often confused with punishment, when, in fact, the two are essentially opposite (i.e., they have opposite effects on behavior). Negative reinforcement leads to an increase in behavior and punishment leads to a decrease in behavior. Further, negative reinforcement is experienced by the person exhibiting the behavior as favorable, whereas punishment is experienced as unfavorable. In other words, to the extent that it is reasonable to say that people want an aversive situation to end, it is reasonable to say that people enjoy receiving negative reinforcement because that's what it is—the termination of an aversive situation.

Another consequence condition important to understanding behavior and in planning FBA-based interventions is *extinction*. Extinction is the decrease in a behavior that occurs when a reinforcer is no longer available contingent upon behavior. For example, if a student has been receiving peer attention for making inappropriate comments, but then demonstrates a decrease in the inappropriate comments when his peers begin to ignore him (i.e., not provide attention), then this can be said to be an example of extinction.

Table 2.2 summarizes the relationship between positive and negative reinforcement and positive and negative punishment.

Setting Events

Although the traditional three-term contingency from Figure 2.1 only includes antecedents, behaviors, and consequence, we also know that a fourth term is important in our understanding of the controlling relationship between behavior and the environment. *Setting events* are conditions that set up the likelihood that a behavior will occur in the presence of its functional antecedent, generally by temporarily altering the value of the consequence associated with it. For example, Carr and Blakeley-Smith (2006) found that illness was a common setting event for children with developmental disabilities whose

Table 2.2 The relationship between positive and negative reinforcement and punishment

		Effect of Consequence on Behavior	
		Behavior Increase	Behavior Decrease
	Add a stimulus	**Positive Reinforcement**	**Positive Punishment**
CHANGE IN CONDITIONS	Remove a stimulus	**Negative Reinforcement**	**Negative Punishment**
	No stimulus added (discontinuing a previously added stimulus)		**Extinction**

behavior was maintained by negative reinforcement. These children were far more motivated to escape various tasks when they were ill than when they weren't ill. Other common setting events include lack of sleep, poor rapport with a child, conflict at home or with peers, and recent negative social interactions. When these setting events occur, we can assume that a child's problem behavior will temporarily be more likely than when the setting events do not occur. The three-term contingency with setting events included is illustrated in Figure 2.2. In terms of relevance for FBAs and planning interventions, it is important to note that the effects of setting events differ across children. Some children will be greatly affected by lack of sleep, whereas others will be minimally affected by lack of sleep. It is important to learn through an FBA which setting events are most relevant to the problem behavior.

Within the functional model of behavior, we understand that everyone demonstrates different behavior in response to different situations based on their history of interacting with these situations. Some students have found that telling inappropriate jokes is a good way to get attention from peers, while others have learned that telling inappropriate jokes gets them into trouble with their parents. Some students learn that the best time to tell an inappropriate joke is when there are many peers around, while other students

Setting Event ➡ Antecedent ➡ Behavior ➡ Consequence

FIGURE 2.2 The relationship of setting events to the three-term contingency.

have learned that the best time to tell an inappropriate joke is when only one trusted friend is nearby. Although these unique learning histories are important when trying to understand how the problem began, our focus in a functional model of behavior is always going to be on what is currently happening in the environment that is predicting (via setting events and antecedents) and maintaining (via positive and negative reinforcers) problem behaviors. Hence, it is often stated that the functional model of behavior is very present-focused when compared to other models used to help students with their problems.

Functional Behavioral Assessment: Definition and Relevance across Tiers

FBA is a process for identifying the environmental conditions that predict and maintain problem behavior (O'Neill et al., 1997). This definition highlights the fact that FBA is not a specific set of procedures, but rather a process for which multiple specific procedures could be utilized. For example, interviews can provide useful information about the antecedents and consequences of behavior and are therefore useful in an FBA. However, interview data are more prone to bias because they are indirect. Therefore, other data, such as direct observations and archival data, can also be used to increase confidence in an FBA. The critical question in determining whether an FBA has been completed is whether the environmental variables that predict and maintain problem behavior have been clearly and correctly identified. Using the terminology from the functional model of behavior, we can say more precisely that an FBA is the process of identifying the antecedents, setting events, and consequences of problem behavior.

The primary outcome of an FBA is a precision hypothesis statement. A *precision hypothesis statement* is a statement that summarizes the antecedents, behaviors, and consequences for a specific problem behavior. The specifics of how to write a precision hypothesis statement will be reviewed in Chapters 3, 5, and 6 that address specific Tier 1, Tier 2, and Tier 3 FBAs.

The purpose for conducting an FBA is to develop an effective intervention. In fact, there is no logical reason to conduct an FBA if it is not used to inform intervention. Unfortunately, FBAs are often completed without being tied to interventions. We find it an all-to-common experience that FBAs are completed by school staff as part of a legal mandate in special education disability determinations, but are not considered when writing BIPs or IEPs. This is an unfortunate situation, given that a process for developing interventions from FBAs has been well-established and that the literature reviewed at the end of this chapter makes clear that behavior interventions are most effective when based on FBAs. Therefore, this book will address the process of connecting FBA information to interventions at each of the tiers.

The Three-tiered Model of Functional Behavioral Assessment

Much has been written about using FBA in schools since it was codified into education law through the 1997 IDEA legislation (Ervin et al., 2001), and prior to that, much was written about the relationship of FBA to the general management of behavior problems among individuals with disabilities (Hanley, Iwata, & McCord, 2003). However, using FBA to inform interventions in tiers 1 and 2 of a prevention model is a relatively new idea about which very little has been written. The purpose of this book, then, is to expand what is currently known about FBA and apply it to the three-tiered model of prevention.

The three-tiered model of preventing problem behavior is based largely on Walker et al.'s (1996) challenge to the field of education to decrease serious problem behaviors by reorganizing the ways in which behavior services are provided. They argued that a three-tiered system of allocating resources that coincides with a discontinuation of reactive and punitive procedures would be the most efficient system for improving behavior in schools. They suggested that most students could be supported with simple prevention efforts, at-risk students could be supported by more structured supports, and students with significant behavior problems could be supported by individualized, comprehensive services. FBA can support of all these efforts while reducing the need for reactive and punitive procedures.

Some aspects of FBA remain stable across tiers, including the general definition of the process, its purpose, and its outcome, each of which were described above. So, at each level, we will employ a process of identifying the antecedents, setting events, and consequences of problem behavior (definition); develop precision hypothesis statements (outcome); and use the results to inform intervention (purpose).

Alternatively, there are aspects that differ significantly across tiers, including the populations that are served and the specific data that are gathered to develop the precision hypothesis statements that inform interventions. At Tier 1, FBA is applied to understanding the behaviors of all students in a school. This requires a unique set of data since it is impractical to directly observe each student or to interview every teacher about the students' behaviors. So, Tier 1 FBA focuses on efficient sources of data about the behaviors, antecedents, setting events, and consequences of all students. In specific, we will describe how to use office discipline referral information to develop precision hypothesis statements that inform Tier 1 interventions.

At Tier 2, FBA is applied to understand the behavior of a group of students who did not respond to the FBA-based interventions in Tier 1 and whose behavior puts them at risk for poor outcomes. But because the focus at Tier 2 is on matching at-risk students to existing package interventions, rather than developing individualized behavior plans, it is not be necessary to conduct an intensive FBA. Instead, we will focus our directions on efficient methods of collecting Tier 2 FBA information, such as using existing data from Tier 1 and brief interviews.

At Tier 3, FBA focuses on the behavior of students with significant behavior problems who did not respond to Tier 1 or Tier 2 interventions. The goal is to develop an intense and effective individualized BIP. So, it is necessary at Tier 3 to gather as much quality FBA information as possible. This includes the data gathered at Tier 1 and Tier 2 and new information from structured interviews and direct observations. The three-tiered model of FBA, with focus data used, interventions developed, and populations served, is summarized in Figure 2.3.

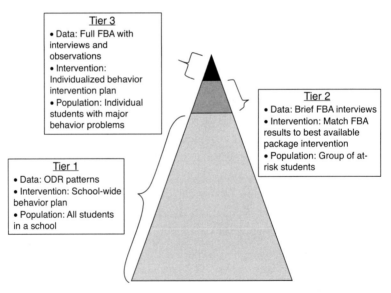

FIGURE 2.3 A summary of the data collected, interventions developed, and populations served that differentiate each of the three tiers of functional behavioral assessment.

Functional Behavioral Assessment

Research Supporting Functional Behavioral Assessments

The research literature supporting the use of a functional model of behavior in schools is extensive. In 2001, Ervin and her colleagues reviewed 100 published studies on FBAs in schools that led to behavior interventions and found that all of the studies supported the use of FBA in schools. However, at the time, they noted that there were very few examples of FBAs conducted for problem behaviors that occur at low rates, or that occur with high-frequency disabilities. This literature has since been expanded to address many of these issues, and it is now generally considered that FBA is an effective tool for use with most behaviors for most populations of school-aged children and adolescents (Filter & Horner, 2009; McIntosh, Brown, & Borgmeier, 2008; Stahr, Cushing, Lane, & Fox., 2006).

The critical issue in examining the importance of FBAs when developing interventions is the extent to which interventions that are based on FBAs are more effective than interventions that are not based on FBAs. Three recent experimental studies have made this comparison, and all three found that interventions based on FBAs were significantly more effective than were interventions not based on FBAs (Filter & Horner, 2009; Ingram et al., 2005; Newcomer & Lewis, 2004).

In addition to clearly leading to effective outcomes for students, the use of FBAs has also led to a decrease in the use of punishment-based interventions. Pelios, Morren, Tesch, and Axelrod (1999) found that, since the earliest applications of FBA technology (which is generally credited to Iwata, Dorsey, Slifer, Bauman, and Richman [1982]), the treatment of aggression and self-injurious behavior has shifted from the predominance of punishment procedures to a more recent predominance of reinforcement-based procedures. This is because FBA allows us to determine what reinforcers are currently maintaining the problem behavior, so that those reinforcers can be used instead to maintain appropriate behaviors. When you don't know what is maintaining a problem behavior, you are more likely to choose a punishment-based procedure to reduce the problem, even though it is generally agreed that reinforcement procedures are ethically preferable to punishment procedures (Miltenberger, 2004).

It is important to note that the research on FBA supports its use with a wide range of behaviors. However, it is easy to misapply the concept of behavior to mean *disorders*, which is a medically contrived cluster of symptoms, some of which are overt behaviors. FBAs and associated interventions can be effective in improving a number of behaviors associated with various externalizing disorders (e.g., attention-deficit hyperactivity disorder, conduct disorder), but FBAs are more difficult to apply to internalizing disorders (e.g., depression, anxiety) because many of the behaviors included in these disorders are observable only by the person experiencing them (e.g., feelings of inadequacy, suicidal thoughts). Although FBAs can be used with internalizing disorders, the research in this area is still underdeveloped for use with school-aged children. As a result, this book focuses on overt behaviors that may or may not be associated with various disorders, but it will not focus on disorders in the broader sense.

Infrastructure for Supporting Functional Behavioral Assessments

Now that we have established that FBAs improve the quality and effectiveness of interventions for problem behavior, we turn to the conditions in a school that support the use of FBAs. Although more research in this area will be necessary, Medley, Little, and Akin-Little (2008) found that the quality of Tier 3 FBAs was significantly higher in schools that were implementing school-wide positive behavior support (SWPBS) than in schools that were not implementing SWPBS. This fits perfectly with the logic of SWPBS, which is a systems-level approach to preventing problem behavior based on the functional model of behavior. One of the historical motivators for the development of SWPBS was the need to develop systems that supported and maintained quality behavioral practices, including FBAs and behavior intervention plans (Colvin, Kameenui, & Sugai, 1993). Given the data from Medley et al. and the logic of SWPBS, we take the position that FBAs and their corresponding BIPs are most likely to be implemented with fidelity in schools that are implementing the critical features of SWPBS. This is not meant to imply that schools that are not implementing SWPBS should not pursue the use of FBA in a three-tiered model. Rather, our point is that the SWPBS model addresses a number of features that any school could implement to increase the likelihood of sustained implementation, and its basic features are reviewed here. For a more detailed description of SWPBS, see Sprague and Horner (2006) or Sugai and Horner (2002), or visit the website www.pbis.org.

Staff Commitment

Staff commitment to systems change is critical before implementing systems change. A general rule of thumb is that 80% staff commitment is sufficient for initial implementation. This should include a commitment to support the behaviors of *all* students in a school. This will be relevant for conducting

FBAs across all three tiers. A good way to encourage staff commitment is to invest in staff development presentations for the whole school regarding the changes that may take place. It is also helpful to have staff from another school that has already successfully implemented the systems changes (e.g., SWPBS and FBAs across all three tiers) communicate with the school that may adopt the systems change. After this initial exposure phase, a vote should be taken to determine the percentage of staff that are committed to the change. If the 80% criterion is met, we can then assume that it is a good time to begin implementing the new system. If the criterion is not met, we recommend spending additional time in the readiness phase before implementation.

Team-based Approach

Behavior issues in a school, including the planning and implementing of FBAs and BIPs, should be managed by a team in the school. Although the social worker may have more behavioral expertise than most other professionals in the school, the social worker's contribution should be to the team, rather than as an independent expert. Minimally, the team should be comprised of teachers, an administrator, and someone with behavioral expertise (e.g., social worker, school psychologist, EBD teacher). This team is responsible for gathering all of the data for FBAs in Tier 1, Tier 2, and Tier 3. The team also develops BIPs based on the FBAs and monitors their implementations and effects. We recommend that this team serve as the school's general team for addressing all behavior issues, rather than functioning like an IEP team, in which the membership changes based on the specific case. The details of how the team manages the process of FBAs and interventions will be described in later chapters.

Continuum of Behavior Services

As you move up from Tier 1 through Tier 3 within a continuum of behavior services, the intensity of FBAs increases. But this assumes that a three-tiered system of services is in place: For three tiers of FBA to have value, there should be three corresponding tiers of services that FBA can inform. For example, Tier 1 services within SWPBS involve teaching behavior expectations to all students and then providing reinforcement when students demonstrate those behavior expectations. Once these basic Tier 1 services are in place, the details of how to continuously improve behavior at this level can be informed by a low-intensity Tier 1 FBA that involves reviewing whole-school behavior data for patterns of antecedents and consequences (because Tier 1 services, by definition, involve all students rather than individual students). Tier 2 behavior services are for students at risk of significant problems and would generally include efficient and effective package interventions. When multiple intervention packages are available for students in Tier 2, then Tier 2 FBAs that inform group interventions can be conducted. Tier 3 behavior services generally include individualized behavior plans for students with severe behavior problems. Once a school has a process for providing these individualized services (which often correspond with special education services), the Tier 3 FBAs that will inform the details of the individualized interventions can be conducted.

Data-based Decision Making

The information that is gleaned from FBAs at all three tiers leads to the development of strong interventions at each tier, but only if the school has a mechanism for making decisions based on data. In many schools, data are collected on a regular basis, but no process has been established for making decisions based on those data. For example, almost all schools collect office discipline referral data, but many schools suffer from the "shoebox" tendency for data storage and use (i.e., the referral data are literally stored in a shoebox). When the administrators of shoebox schools are asked if they have discipline data in the form of office discipline referrals, the answer will be "yes." But when asked to describe what they have learned from those data, at best they often respond, "We have a lot of them." These schools have not reviewed the data for decision making. They have not considered whether there is any information about the environmental conditions that predict or maintain behavior (e.g., location, time of day, motivation). It is also not uncommon for schools to conduct individual FBAs in Tier 3 but then put the data in a file (i.e., shoebox) and not revisit it when it comes time to develop interventions.

The behavior team described above is the context in which good, data-based decisions should be made, but it is not sufficient to simply have a team. Data-based decisions are made within routines. Teams need to establish a regular meeting routine that includes time dedicated to reviewing data, modifying action plans, and writing or modifying individual behavior plans based on those data. From our experience, this works best when behavior is the topic covered in the first 15 to 30 minutes of each meeting. This ensures that the team is not side-tracked by other issues. Instead, the "other" issues become those that are dealt with only after data-based decisions have been made.

Administrative Commitment

There is an old saying that if you want to know what someone's values are, see where they spend their money and time. This is particularly relevant when working with school administrators. An administrator who values data-based behavior decisions in the school (including FBA across the tiers) will have committed a portion of the budget to supporting these activities and will be a member of the behavior team In addition to the potential financial benefit of having administrators on board, they can also be helpful because their position of authority can be used to support behavior services when working with the staff. This influence can also be used to focus on the small percentage of staff who may not have bought into the process. So, it is a positive situation when the school administrator is already involved in FBA and behavior services. If the administrator is not involved, it would be a good use of energy to invest in gaining support before committing to an ambitious, three-tiered system of FBA-based behavior services.

Summary

In this chapter, we reviewed the general logic underlying FBA, the legal foundations of FBA, the application of FBA in a three-tiered model of prevention, and research and systems that support FBA. To summarize, FBA is a process that leads to effective behavior interventions by identifying the setting events and antecedents that predict problem behavior and the consequences that maintain it. This process can be applied to individual students in Tier 3, to targeted groups of at-risk students in Tier 2, and to all students within a school in Tier 1. In the remaining chapters, we will review the specifics of conducting FBAs and developing interventions at each tier.

3

▩▩▩

Tier 1 Functional Behavioral Assessment

School social workers often think of FBAs as filling out antecedent-behavior-consequence (ABC) forms, conducting direct observations, and discussing the findings in a special education meeting. This process is visible at the Tier 2 and Tier 3 levels, with increasing rigor. However, at Tier 1, the FBA uses a briefer format and is applied school-wide. FBAs at Tier 1 utilize the functional model of behavior based on the identification of problem behaviors and their setting events, antecedents, and consequences. These FBAs lead to the development of a precision hypothesis statement and serve the purpose of developing interventions. In contrast to FBA at other tiers, FBAs at Tier 1 apply to all students in the school and use school-wide data, such as office discipline referrals, to plan school-wide behavior interventions and monitor outcomes. By focusing on all students, Tier 1 FBAs take on a broader context and application, as opposed to the individual student focus of Tier 2 and Tier 3 FBAs.

Research suggests that FBA is most effective when applied early, as a preventative procedure, before problem behaviors become entrenched (Scott, Liaupsin, Nelson, & McIntyre, 2005). Clark and Alvarez (2010) explain that Tier 1 encompasses all students and thus reduces the number of targeted group interventions and intensive individualized interventions needed in a school. In other words, by making small changes, based on FBA information, that impact all students, schools can reduce the intense resource investment required to provide Tier 2 and Tier 3 supports.

As with all tiers, the *definition* of functional behavioral assessment (FBA) at Tier 1 is a process of identifying the antecedents and consequences of problem behavior, the *outcome* of FBA at Tier 1 is the development of a precision hypothesis statement, and the *purpose* of FBA at Tier 1 is to develop effective interventions.

When conducting a Tier 1 FBA, the population served is all students in a school, the data collected are office discipline referrals, and the interventions developed are school-wide behavior intervention plans (BIPs).

Tier 1 Functional Behavioral Data
Functional Data

When conducting an FBA at any tier, it is important to identify the setting events, antecedents, and consequences that maintain problem behavior. At Tier 1, this involves collecting data on the behaviors of all students in a school, as well as the setting events, antecedents, and consequences of these behaviors in order to develop school-wide interventions. Since antecedents and setting events are such similar concepts (i.e., both generally occur before behavior and affect the likelihood of behavior) and are difficult to delineate without significant analysis of individual situations, we will combine these two variables when describing school-wide FBA processes at Tier 1. Table 3.1 provides examples of some of the setting events/antecedents, behaviors, and consequences that could be identified in Tier 1. Setting events/antecedents are divided into locations, times of day, and activities. Although this is not meant to be an exhaustive list, these are broad, school-wide antecedents that could be efficiently manipulated and may be relevant to the behavior of many students. The problem behaviors in this list are those that are just as relevant to individual students as they would be to large groups of students. In essence, there is no differentiation between school-wide behaviors and individual student behaviors except for their frequency in the larger group. When conducting Tier 1 FBAs, the school team should be focused on behaviors that occur with high frequency in the school and are not attributable to just one or two students. The consequences in Table 3.1 are the same

Table 3.1 Examples of setting events/antecedents, behaviors, and consequences in Tier 1

Setting Events/ Antecedents	Behaviors	Consequences
Location: • Classroom • Hallway • Lunchroom Time of day: • Before school • Afternoon Activities: • Instruction • Unstructured activities	Bullying Tardiness Verbal abuse Defiance	Obtain: • Peer attention • Adult attention • Activity • Tangible Escape from: • Peer attention • Adult attention • Activity • Tangible

consequences that would be identified in any tier and the same as those described in Chapter 2. The trick to gathering these data in Tier 1 is to develop a process whereby each behavior incident in a school is recorded not only as behavior, but is also recorded to include information about the setting events/ antecedents and the consequences. In the next section, we will describe how office discipline referrals (ODRs) can serve this purpose with only a few simple modifications.

Sources of Data

The FBA data gathered at Tier 1 should be simple and efficient. These data should also be inclusive of all major behavior incidents that occur in a school. In traditional FBAs designed for Tier 2 and Tier 3 issues, FBA data are collected via direct observation or interviews about behavior incidents. This process works well for individual students but is neither simple nor efficient for school-wide, Tier 1 purposes. Instead, we recommend that schools use already-existing school data, which can include information about major behavior incidents or ODRs. Although other existing data sources can be used to supplement Tier 1 FBAs, such as attendance records and suspensions/expulsions, ODRs will be reviewed as a primary option since they can be easily modified to include the

Functional Behavioral Assessment

most relevant information about setting events/antecedents, behaviors, and consequences at the school-wide level.

Office Discipline Referrals

The first issue to consider when using ODRs for Tier 1 FBAs is the accuracy and reliability of ODR data. Although ODRs have been demonstrated to be useful in Tier 1 decision-making (Irvin, Tobin, Sprague, Sugai, & Vincent, 2004) and accurate in predicting future rates of ODRs for groups of students (McIntosh et al., 2010), they have value only when schools have invested effort to make them valuable. The problem with ODRs is that they are not a direct measure of student behavior. Instead, they also reflect the reporting behavior of the teacher, which can vary significantly from one teacher to the next, and the accuracy of the data entry process. In other words, ODR data may not reflect behavior in a school accurately if teachers are not recording ODRs for the same behaviors in the same situations, or if the person entering the ODRs into a database is not careful about the recording process. Ultimately, teacher consistency when documenting ODRs is often a serious issue for schools. Further, school administration may not agree with teachers as to which behaviors should be documented on an ODR and which behaviors shouldn't be documented. So, all of these pitfalls need to be addressed before using ODR data for Tier 1 FBAs and school-wide decision making.

Another issue with using ODRs for Tier 1 FBAs is the degree to which ODRs include information about setting events/antecedents and consequences. Schools vary widely in the data that they include in ODRs. They vary so widely, in fact, that we have worked with some schools that collect no ODR data and others that collect ODR data using very clear lists of antecedents and consequences. The most common pattern, though, seems to be schools that include information about the behavior, but very little information that could be interpreted as setting events/antecedents or consequences. Therefore, if a school intends to pursue Tier 1 FBAs, then it will need to develop referral forms that include relevant information. An example of an ODR form that includes information about setting events/antecedents (e.g., location, time of day, others involved) and consequences (described as "possible motivation") is included in Figure 3.1.

To address the two major issues of accuracy/consistency in ODRs and the inclusion of relevant functional information in ODRs, we recommend the following steps. First, develop an agreement between administration

Office Referral Form

Name: _____

Date: _____ **Time:** _____

Teacher: _____

Grade: K 1 2 3 4 5 6 7 8

Referring staff: _____

Location

☐ Playground ☐ Library
☐ Cafeteria ☐ Bathroom
☐ Hallway ☐ Arrival/Dismissal
☐ Classroom ☐ Other _____

Minor problem behavior	Major problem behavior	Possible motivation
☐ Inappropriate language ☐ Physical contact ☐ Defiance ☐ Disruption ☐ Dress code ☐ Property misuse ☐ Tardy ☐ Electronic violation ☐ Other _____	☐ Abusive language ☐ Fighting/Physical aggression ☐ Overt defiance ☐ Harassment/Bullying ☐ Dress code ☐ Tardy ☐ Inappropriate display aff. ☐ Electronic violation ☐ Lying/Cheating ☐ Skipping class ☐ Other	☐ Obtain peer attention ☐ Obtain adult attention ☐ Obtain items/activities ☐ Avoid peer(s) ☐ Avoid adult ☐ Avoid task or activity ☐ Don't know ☐ Other _____
Administrative decision		
☐ Loss of privilege ☐ Time in office ☐ Conference with student ☐ Parent contact	☐ Individualized instruction ☐ In-school suspension (___hours/days) ☐ Out of school suspension (___days) ☐ Other _____	

Others involved in incident: ☐ None ☐ Peers ☐ Staff ☐ Teacher ☐ Substitute
☐ Unknown ☐ Other

Other comments:

_____

☐ I need to talk to the students' teacher   ☐ I need to talk to the administrator

Parent signature: _____ **Date:** _____

All minors are filed with classroom teacher. Three minors equal a major.
All majors require administrator consequence, parent contact, and signature.

FIGURE 3.1 Sample office discipline referral (ODR) form that includes information about setting events/antecedents and consequences. Retrieved from www. swis.org and reproduced with permission from Educational and Community Supports, University of Oregon.

and staff as to which behaviors will be documented and which will not. This should also include an agreement about which behaviors will be referred to the office and which will not. It doesn't need to be the case that all documented behaviors will be referred to the office. For example, a school could decide to document both minor behavior violations and major behavior

Functional Behavioral Assessment

violations but only refer the major violations to the office. The minor violations would then be handled in the classroom or setting in which they occurred. Regardless of the approach decided upon, it is critical to FBA data purposes that an agreement is reached about which behavior violations will be documented. This agreement should be written as a permanent document that describes the process of documenting behavior violations on ODRs.

After gaining agreement about documenting behaviors, the school should then develop ODR forms that include a list of these agreed-upon behaviors and lists of setting event/antecedents and consequences. We recommend lists as opposed to blank entry spaces in which to write behaviors, setting events/antecedents, and consequences because checked boxes or circled items on lists can be entered into a database as specific categories that will make reporting, graphing, and decision making possible. The ODR example from Figure 3.1 incorporates the list format. Another advantage of lists is that they can actually increase consistency in documenting behaviors because, if the teacher or staff member does not see the observed behavior on the ODR form, then she or he knows that it is not supposed to be documented on that form. Conversely, if the observed behavior is on the ODR form, then the teacher or staff member knows that it is a behavior to be documented on that form.

Finally, after deciding which behaviors will be documented and developing forms that include all relevant functional information, teachers and staff need to be trained in the new ODR process. After initial training, the forms themselves should facilitate appropriate use of ODRs by clearly illustrating which behavior should be documented and which setting events/antecedents and consequences should be recorded.

Once a school has dealt with these ODR issues, all staff in the school will be collecting FBA data that can be used for Tier 1 decision making. The next steps will be for the school team to use the data to develop precision hypothesis statements about behavior problems in the school and then to develop and monitor school-wide interventions based on the data.

Summarizing Tier 1 Functional Behavioral Assessment Data

After a school has invested in the process of gathering meaningful and accurate ODR data, the school team can begin using the data for Tier 1 FBAs. This begins by summarizing the ODR data into efficient information about setting events/antecedents, behaviors, and consequences. One model that has been developed for this process is often described as "The Big Five" data model (Illinois PBIS network, 2010; Office of Special Education Programs [OSEP] Center on Positive Behavioral Interventions and Supports, 2004). The Big Five are defined by the Illinois PBIS network (2010) as graphs of the following data:

- Average referrals per day per month
- Referrals by problem behavior
- Referrals by location
- Referrals by time
- Referrals by student (Illinois PBIS Network, 2010, item 6).

We will add to this list by including a graph of motivation for the most frequent problem behavior, and we coin the phrase "The Big Six." We will describe The Big Six and give examples for each below.

Further, we recommend that schools create these graphs of ODR data using the School-Wide Information System (SWIS; May et al., 2000). SWIS is a web-based database for entering ODR data, and for quickly and efficiently creating graphs that can be used for decision making. SWIS is designed to create Big Five graphs and other custom graphs of ODR data, including the motivation for the most frequent problem behavior that we advocate as the sixth important input. More information about SWIS can be found at www.swis.org. Although SWIS is designed to create these graphs very efficiently, schools can create similar graphs using their databases with appropriate technological support.

Average Referrals per Day per Month

A graph of average referrals per day per month is a summary of the general level of problem behavior in a school over time. By focusing on the "per day per month" metric, the data for each month are directly comparable to any other month and not affected by the number of days in a month. It can be used to answer the basic question, "Do we have a problem?" by comparing levels of ODRs over time (i.e., "Is there a recent increase in referrals?") or by comparing school ODR levels to the national norms (i.e., "Does our school have more referrals than would be expected in comparable schools?"). National ODR norms are updated annually on the website www.swis.org under the *User Resources* link and are delineated by grade levels in a school. For example, the 2009–2010 ODR data for major referrals (not minor referrals) indicate that K–6 schools average 0.22 referrals per 100 students

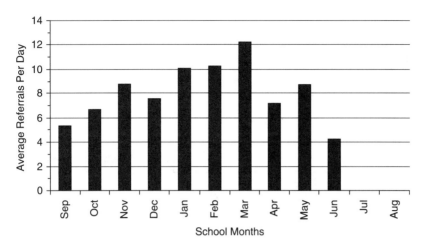

FIGURE 3.2 Example of a high school's graph of average referrals per day per month. Graph generated using the School-Wide Information System (www. swis.org).

per day. So, a K–6 school with 300 students in 2009–2010 would be expected to have 0.66 referrals every day. If a K–6 school with 300 students was averaging 1.3 ODRs per day according to their average referrals per day per month graph, then the school would likely have a problem with behavior that would be important to address with a Tier 1 FBA process. An example of a graph of a high school's referrals per day per month is provided in Figure 3.2. This particular graph demonstrates a pattern of increasing ODRs from fall into winter, but a decreasing trend into the spring. This is a pattern that could be expected by a team that identified a need to conduct a Tier 1 FBA in late autumn and then went on to implement some FBA-based interventions during the winter to decrease problem behavior in the school.

Referrals by Problem Behavior

A graph that depicts referrals by problem behavior informs the school team as to which behaviors represent the biggest problem in the school, thereby clarifying the behavior in the setting event/antecedent, behavior, consequence model at Tier 1. An example of a graph of referrals by problem behavior is presented in Figure 3.3. The graph indicates that the most commonly occurring problem behavior in the example high school is disrespect. Sometimes, no one problem behavior will clearly occur more often than other problem behaviors; in this case, the school should focus on lowering all problem behaviors rather than concentrating on a particular problem behavior.

Tier 1 Functional Behavioral Assessment *41*

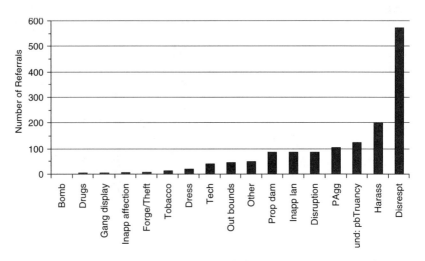

FIGURE 3.3 Example of a high school's graph of referrals by problem behavior. Graph generated using the School-Wide Information System (www.swis.org).

Referrals by Location

The locations in which behavioral violations are occurring provide good antecedent information. For example, if a disproportionate number of ODRs are coming from the hallway, then a team can deduce that something about the hallway setting is triggering or facilitating problem behavior. Unfortunately, information about location of ODRs does not provide enough detail to determine what it is about the location that is precipitating problem behavior (e.g., lack of supervision, students needing to walk quickly to classes that are far away), but we know that changes should be made in that location. A quick caveat to the use of location in decision making is that teams need to consider the relative amount of time that students naturally spend in each location in order to determine whether the number of ODRs from a location are disproportionate to the time spent in those locations. For example, students would be expected to spend 60% of their day in the classroom; so, if 40% of referrals are coming from the classroom, then this does not imply that classroom behavior is the most significant predictor of problem behavior. Conversely, if 25% of the referrals are coming from the playground, but students only spend 10% of their time on the playground, then this would suggest that the playground is a significant predictor of problem behavior. An example of a graph of referrals by location is presented in Figure 3.4. In this graph, approximately 55% of referrals are coming from the classroom and about 15% are coming from the hallways, so this is a situation in which

Functional Behavioral Assessment

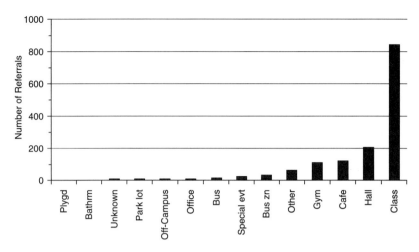

FIGURE 3.4 Example of a high school's graph of referrals by location. Graph
generated using the School-Wide Information System (www.swis.org).

the referral rates closely match the actual time spent in each setting.
The likely implication of this situation would be that general location is not
a strong predictor of problem behavior in the school.

Referrals by Time

Determining the time of day during which behavioral violations occur
can provide more clarity to the antecedents to problem behavior. As was the
case with referrals by location, this information does not necessarily explain

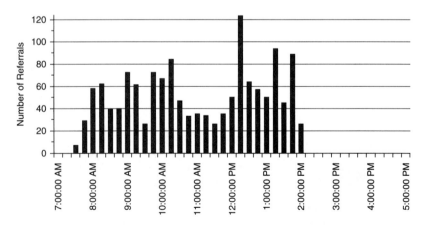

FIGURE 3.5 Example of a high school's graph of referrals by time. Graph generated
using the School-Wide Information System (www.swis.org).

what it is about this antecedent that is directly and functionally related to the behavior. However, it can be the basis for reasonable hypotheses. For example, if ODRs are most often occurring in the classroom, but we note that they occur most often shortly before lunch, as is the case in the example from Figure 3.5, then the team could infer that students are becoming hungry before lunch and acting out in the classroom. In this case, the hunger would be acting as a setting event to the problem behavior, and we could expect that—if our hypothesis is correct—ODRs would decrease if we started lunch a little earlier or if there was some way to provide brief snacks earlier in the day.

Referrals by Student

One of the important questions to ask when using school-wide ODR data to conduct an FBA of student behavior is whether the problem is better explained as being pervasive and school-wide, or if the school's problems are better understood as being the result of the problem behaviors of a small group of students. If the problem is a small group of students rather than a situation in which many students have just a few referrals, then the focus would shift from analyzing and changing antecedents and consequences in the whole school to conducting individual student FBAs and providing FBA-based interventions for these specific students. In other words, this would be a signal to move up to a Tier 2 level of FBA and FBA-based interventions,

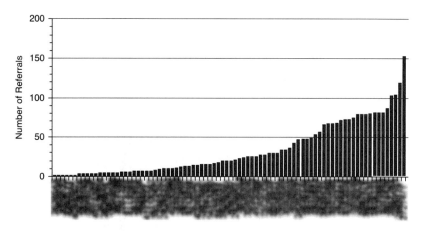

FIGURE 3.6 Example of a graph of referrals by students from a school for students with significant behavioral needs. The tightly clustered text along the x-axis shows the students' identification numbers. Graph generated using the School-Wide Information System (www.swis.org).

Functional Behavioral Assessment

which are explained in further detail later in this chapter and in Chapter 4. Figure 3.6 depicts an example from a school designed for students with significant behavioral needs. The example indicates that many students in the school have one or more ODRs, so it is likely that a school-wide problem exists that should be addressed by a Tier 1 FBA process. However, there are also several students who appear to be in need of additional support, so a Tier 2 and/or Tier 3 FBA process would be appropriate for those students with multiple referrals. An example of how to move from Tier 1 to Tier 2 and Tier 3 is provided at the end this example, and more information about Tier 2 and Tier 3 FBA processes are described in Chapters 5 and 6.

Referrals by Motivation for Most Frequent Problem Behavior

As discussed earlier, ODR information is most useful to an FBA process when it includes information about the motivation/consequences of behaviors that are referred, thus completing the setting event/antecedent, behavior, consequence model of FBA. Therefore, we recommend adding this sixth graph to the Big Five to create the Tier 1 FBA Big Six. Although a graph that shows general information about the motivation of all behaviors documented with ODRs could be useful, we recommend creating a more specific graph of motivation that is based on the most frequently occurring problem behaviors. To accomplish this, the graph of motivation created would be limited to only those behaviors that are most frequent, according to the referrals by problem

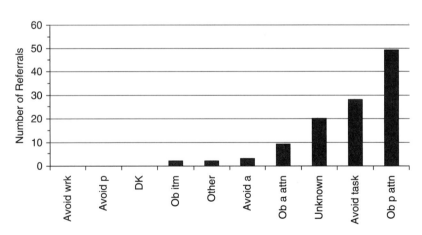

FIGURE 3.7 Example of a high school's graph of referrals by motivation for the behavior of disrespect. Graph generated using the School-Wide Information System (www.swis.org).

behavior graph created earlier. An example of a graph of the motivation for disrespect in a school is provided in Figure 3.7. This example indicates that the most common motivation perceived by those completing the ODRs was "obtain peer attention." One intervention that a school could consider for this situation would be to arrange for students to get peer attention for appropriate behavior rather than for disrespect. This could be accomplished by arranging a positive peer reporting system wherein students provide reward tickets to other students when they observe them demonstrating the school's behavior expectations. For more information on positive peer reporting, see Skinner, Neddenriep, Robinson, Ervin, and Jones (2002).

Other Information
The Big Six graphs provide good information for beginning an analysis of setting events/antecedents, behaviors, and consequences in a school. However, in some cases, it can be useful to analyze other sources of information. For example, ODR by location data can be evaluated with more specificity if a team creates a graph of ODRs from classrooms, arranged by teachers. This would indicate whether each teacher is referring approximately equal numbers of students from his or her classroom, or if just a few classrooms are accounting for the majority of the problem. Other potentially useful information from an ODR would include "others involved" (antecedent or consequence), "grade" (who is exhibiting problem behavior), and "administrative decision" (possible maintaining consequence; e.g., suspension as escape). Data other than ODRs can also be used for analyzing setting events/antecedents, behaviors, and consequences if the team believes that multiple sources of information are necessary. However, each of these data sources will need to be reviewed for quality in the same way that ODRs were before they can be used for decision making.

Precision Hypothesis Statements
After reviewing the Big Six ODR data for Tier 1 FBAs, a team should develop a precision hypothesis statement. A precision hypothesis statement is a precise definition of the problem that also describes the setting events, antecedents, and consequences. Although a statement such as "too many referrals" may give you an idea that a problem exists, a statement such as "there were more ODRs for aggression in the cafeteria than last year, and they appear to be motivated by escape from peer attention" gives you more specific and useful information. A precision hypothesis statement at Tier 1 goes beyond the

Developing Tier 1 FBA Precision Hypothesis Statements

Behavior	Students	Location/Time of Day	Motivation	Precision Statement
				1.
				2.
				3.
				4.
				5.

FIGURE 3.8 A form that teams can use to develop Tier 1 FBA precision hypothesis statements.

definition of the problem to include information about antecedents, such as time of day and location, and information about consequences, such as the information gathered from graphs of motivation of most frequent problem behavior. A form is provided to assist in writing a precision hypothesis statement (see Figure 3.8).

Using the form in Figure 3.8, the team begins by summarizing the information from the Big Six separately. This information is then combined into a comprehensive statement about how the setting events, antecedents, behaviors, and consequences relate to one another. The form is designed for multiple hypotheses that could be developed over time based on changing data. For example, the first time that the team reviewed the Big Six data, they would use the first row of the form to create a precision hypothesis statement. Each time the team got together to review the data after that (e.g., monthly), they would create new precision hypotheses as the data warranted. It is not expected that a new precision hypothesis statement will be created every month. Instead, they are developed when the data indicate a need (as evidenced by data from the graph of referrals per day per month) and when the setting events, antecedents, and consequences appear to have changed. An example of a precision hypothesis statement based on the example Big

Example Precision Hypothesis Statement

There are many office discipline referrals for disrespect in the classroom. Many students have been referred, so it appears to be a school-wide problem. There is no clear pattern indicating the time of day that predicts the problem behavior, but it appears to be motivated primarily by obtaining peer attention.

Six graphs presented thus far in this chapter (Figures 3.2 through Figure 3.7) is provided in the box above.

Developing and Monitoring Tier I FBA-based Interventions
Developing Interventions

By clearly identifying the setting events/antecedents, behaviors, and consequences in a precision hypothesis statement, a team is able to identify school variables that could be changed in Tier 1, in order to change student behavior. This is accomplished by developing efficient and logical interventions that could alter the setting events/antecedents and/or consequences. For example, if the problem behavior is occurring on the playground, then alterations to the supervision and rule-teaching on the playground should decrease the problem behavior. If the problem behavior is motivated by escape from peer attention, then the school could teach students more appropriate ways

Tier 1 Behavior Problem	Logical and Efficient Tier 1 Intervention
Fighting in the hallways motivated by escape from peer attention	Increase the amount of supervision in the hallways using active supervision (Colvin, Sugai, Good, & Lee, 1997)
Disruptive behaviors in the classroom motivated by escape from task	Re-teach respect to all students and develop inter-class time out procedure (Nelson & Carr, 1996)
Bullying before school motivated by obtaining peer attention	Ensure that teachers are available before school for supervision and implement bully prevention by teaching students the stop, walk, and talk method (Ross & Horner, 2009; www.pbis.org)

FIGURE 3.9 Example interventions for Tier 1 behavior problems.

Functional Behavioral Assessment

to ask peers to leave them alone. Examples of logical and efficient interventions for several different Tier 1 problems are provided in Figure 3.9. When feasible, we strongly recommend that schools look for examples of published interventions that have been demonstrated empirically to be effective for problems similar to those identified in the precision hypothesis statement.

Action Planning with Goals and Decisions

After Tier 1 FBA-based interventions have been developed, the team should document on an action planning form the intervention details, a plan to measure the effects of the intervention, and data-based decisions about the intervention's continued use. The action planning document provided in Figure 3.10 enhances accountability for Tier 1 processes by ensuring that intervention ideas developed based on FBAs don't end up being just that—ideas. The action plan documentation method is contrasted with the more traditional "meeting minutes" documentation method used by school teams. Meeting minutes are organized around meeting dates, rather than around interventions. The action planning document is one record that is used in every meeting and is organized around intervention decisions. This ensures that intervention ideas developed several meetings ago do not get lost in the

Tier 1 FBA-Based Action Planning

Activity	Expected Outcome	Person Responsible	Begin Date	Review Date	Decision (continue, eliminate, modify)
1.					
2.					
3.					
4.					
5.					

FIGURE 3.10 An action planning form for teams to use when developing and monitoring Tier 1 FBA-based interventions.

paperwork shuffle between meetings. So, teams are encouraged to spend some time at each meeting reviewing the Tier 1 FBA-based action plan (Figure 3.10) and make intervention decisions based on data.

When developing goals (listed as "expected outcomes" on the Tier 1 FBA-based action plan in Figure 3.10), teams should use ODR data as the primary outcome measure because these data can be collected continuously and are sensitive to program-level changes (Irvin et al., 2004). The goal should be written to specify (a) the amount of decrease in ODRs that would be expected (b) for a particular behavior (c) in a particular location (d) by a specified date. For example, if the problem in the school is disrespect in the classroom, then the team could specify that it expects to see a 50% reduction in ODRs for disrespect in the classroom within 2 months.

The Tier 1 action plan also specifies the person responsible for the intervention, a begin date, a review date, and decisions made. By specifying a person responsible for the intervention, it is not expected that he or she will be the person to implement the intervention, but rather that he or she will oversee the implementation of the intervention (i.e., ensure that the elements of the intervention are implemented by those people who should be implementing them). Decisions can be categorized as continue, eliminate, or modify. The process of making decisions based on progress monitoring data is further elaborated in Chapter 4 (see Table 4.1 in particular). In general, an intervention should be continued if it appears to be working in the short term, but not enough time has elapsed to attain the expected outcome; an intervention should be modified if it is not working in the short term, but not enough time has elapsed to attain the expected outcome; and an intervention should be eliminated if it has failed to attain the expected outcome. If an intervention has attained its expected outcome, then it is at the discretion of the team to continue it or gradually fade it out, which is a form of elimination. To make these decisions, the team must review the ODR data specified in the action plan at each meeting until the intervention is discontinued.

Moving from Tier 1 to Tier 2

FBAs conducted at Tier 1 could indicate that the problem involves a small group of students. When the problem appears to involve only a few students, rather than be a systemic issue, then Tier 2 or Tier 3 FBA processes should be considered in addition to the continued use of the Tier 1 FBA process. When targeting a group of students for Tier 2 FBAs, the process begins by reviewing the data that were generated for those students from Tier 1. The process of moving from a Tier 1 FBA process to a Tier 2 FBA process is illustrated using the following case example of a middle school.

Middle School Case Example

This case example involves a suburban middle school with an enrollment of 750 students in grades 7 and 8. The team is reviewing data at the end of the academic year to determine if the current Tier 1 interventions are addressing the needs of all students in the school. Decisions made will be implemented in the following school year.

The middle school behavior team reviewed the Big Six data, beginning with the average number of referrals per day per month (see Figure 3.11). They referred to the most recently available national norms for ODRs available on www.swis.org, which indicated that the median number of ODRs per day was 0.5 per 100 students in grades 6–9. Therefore, this number should be about 3.75 per day for the 750 middle school students in this school. The team found that the number of referrals per day per month was less than the median, except for November, which had an average of 7 per day. The team

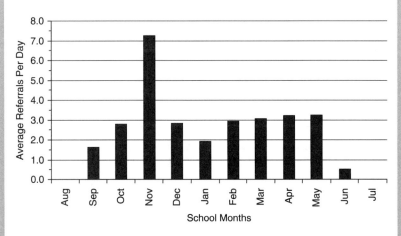

FIGURE 3.11 Case study example of a middle school's office referrals per day per month. Graph generated using the School-Wide Information System (www. swis.org).

decided to brainstorm about why more referrals might occur in November than in any other month of the school year. They also discussed whether the problem was consistent enough to warrant further planning. They ultimately decided that the school was not doing as well as they would like and that they needed to review the remaining Big Six data to understand how to improve behavior in the school.

The team then examined the referrals by problem behavior (see Figure 3.12). The most frequent behavior prompting a referral to the office was disrespect. Aggression, disruption, and inappropriate language were also very common.

The team then looked at the location in which the behaviors were occurring. It is clear in Figure 3.13 that most ODRs were from the classroom. The team then looked at the time when most ODRs occurred (see Figure 3.14). It appeared that ODRs were more likely to occur in the afternoon than in the morning. Although there was no apparent pattern, they were most likely to occur at 3:30 PM.

When the team reviewed the data on referrals by student (Figure 3.15), they discovered that most students had five or fewer referrals during the school year. However, a small group of students

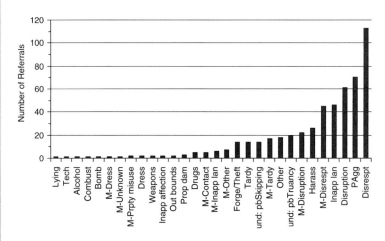

FIGURE 3.12 Case study example of a middle school's referrals by problem behavior. Graph generated using the School-Wide Information System (www. swis.org).

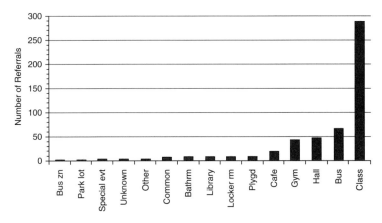

FIGURE 3.13 Case study example of a middle school's referrals by location. Graph generated using the School-Wide Information System (www.swis.org).

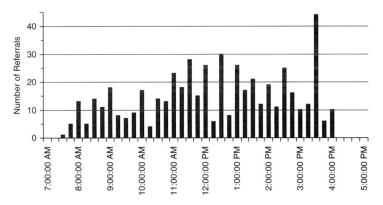

FIGURE 3.14 Case study example of a middle school's referrals by time of day. Graph generated using the School-Wide Information System (www.swis.org).

had 15 or more referrals, and another larger subgroup of students had 10–15 referrals. In this case, it was clear that Tier 2 FBAs should be considered for these students. The team began by examining the data for students with 15 or more discipline referrals. Once this process is complete, they plan to examine data for students with 10–15 discipline referrals.

The team then reviewed the existing data on the function of ODRs for disrespect (see Figure 3.16). The graph indicates that the

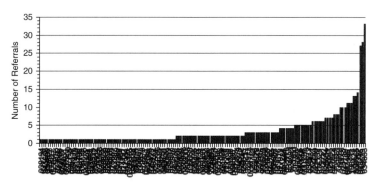

FIGURE 3.15 Case study example of a middle school's referrals by student. Graph generated using the School-Wide Information System (www.swis.org).

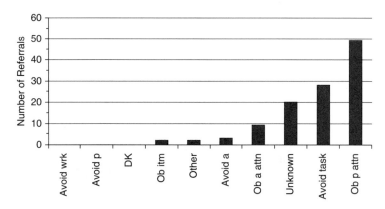

FIGURE 3.16 Case study example of a middle school's referrals by the most commonly occurring behavior of disrespect. Graph generated using the School-Wide Information System (www.swis.org).

most common function for the most frequently occurring problem behavior of disrespect was to obtain peer attention. Avoiding tasks appeared to be the second most common function of disrespect.

After reviewing all of these data, the team decided that, although there are some issues to be addressed at the level of the whole school, they needed to ensure that the many students with multiple ODRs over the past year were supported by a Tier 2 FBA process. Individualized FBAs with rigor that match the level of the Tier 2 FBA process were then planned for those students with 15 or more office discipline referrals. Although it is generally recommended that the Tier 2 FBA process is most appropriate for students with two to seven ODRs, this school decided that it did not have the capacity to conduct a Tier 3 FBA process for so many students. Instead, the school plans to begin to support these students at Tier 2, in hopes that many of them will not require Tier 3 FBA-based services. Information reviewed by the team in Tier 1 will inform this next step. In some cases, there may be justification for a Tier 3 FBA process, which is recommended for students with eight or more ODRs who do not respond to Tier 2 interventions or who demonstrate behavior that is a physical danger to themselves or others.

So, the team decided that each of the students with 15 or more ODRs will need some more individualized FBAs in Tier 2. In Tier 2, each student will receive a brief individual FBA, which includes a review of the existing ODR data for each student from Tier 1 and a brief interview; then, they will be matched to evidenced-based packaged interventions, as described in Chapter 5. It is important to note that the Tier 1 FBA process continues while activities are occurring at Tiers 2 and 3. Ultimately, the team will collect data on antecedents, behaviors, and consequences at all tiers and implement FBA-based interventions for all tiers concurrently.

Summary

FBAs have a place at Tier 1 and can be applied to all students. Naturally occurring data, such as ODRs, are analyzed for patterns of setting events/ antecedents, behaviors, and consequences across a whole school using the Big Six Tier 1 FBA graphs. This information then informs the development of a precision hypothesis statement, which in turn informs the development of a Tier 1 FBA-based intervention action plan. In some cases, Tier 1 data indicate that the behavior problems are not so much a systemic problem as they are a problem with a targeted group of students, in which case the Tier 1 FBA process then moves to a Tier 2 FBA process for that targeted group of students. A fidelity checklist can guide a school-based team in implementing FBAs at Tier 1 (see Figure 3.17).

Tier 1 FBA-Based Intervention Planning and Monitoring
Fidelity Checklist

TASK	DATE COMPLETED
Step 1. Invest in the validity of ODRs as a measure for FBAs by a. Gaining agreement between administration and staff regarding which behaviors are documented and office referred b. Modifying ODR forms to include important information about antecedents and consequences of behavior c. Training all staff on the use of the ODR forms	
Step 2. Collect data on The Big Six (referrals per day per month, referrals by student, referrals by behavior, referrals by location, referrals by time of day, and referrals of motivation for the most commonly occurring problem behavior) using reliable ODRs.	
Step 3. Develop a precision statement using "Tier 1 FBA Precision Statements" form.	
Step 4. For each precision statement, develop an action plan using the "Tier 1 FBA-Based Action Planning" form: a. Develop a logical intervention that should improve behavior based on the precision statement of the problem b. Establish and monitor a goal using the Big Six ODR data	
Step 5. Review data to decide if goal has been met and then decide whether to continue, modify, or eliminate intervention.	
Step 6. Determine whether Tier 1 data indicate that some students are in need of Tier 2 FBA services	

FIGURE 3.17 Tier 1 FBA Fidelity Checklist.

Functional Behavioral Assessment

4

■ ▨ ▨ ▨

Progress Monitoring and Decision Making
for Tier 2 and Beyond

Functional behavioral assessments (FBAs) that inform interventions involve two types of data: functional data and progress monitoring data. Functional data are the information about those environmental factors that predict and maintain the problem behavior. Progress monitoring data are the information about the behavior and how it changes over time in relation to the conditions that we arrange (e.g., interventions). In other words, progress monitoring data doesn't tell us about the antecedents and consequences of behavior, but instead tell us whether behavior is responding to treatment. Progress monitoring data inform our decisions about whether to continue the FBA-based intervention, modify it, or discontinue it. We will spend considerable time in Chapters 5 and 6 discussing how to collect functional data for Tier 2 and Tier 3. This chapter reviews the details of progress monitoring of behavior data over time, as relevant to Tier 2 and Tier 3. We will review the major types of data sources, their strengths and weaknesses, and how to use them to make decisions about behavior supports.

Data Sources for Progress Monitoring

To make quality decisions about behavior, it is necessary to identify measurement tools that have adequate reliability and validity and allow for repeated administration. There are, in fact, many ways of measuring behavior reliably and validly, but most of these methods and tools are not designed to be readministered over a short period of time and therefore are not appropriate for progress monitoring. For example, behavior rating scales such as the Behavior Assessment System for Children, Second Edition

(Reynolds & Kamphaus, 2004) are often used for making special education placement decisions because they are have adequate reliability and validity. They are also efficient for making placement decisions because they can be scored fairly quickly after teachers or caregivers complete them. However, they are not designed to be readministered repeatedly over a short period of time (Watson & Wickstrom, 2004) because of their length and the latency between the actual occurrence of those behaviors and the time that the ratings occur. Therefore, behavior rating scales are poor candidates for progress monitoring in an FBA framework.

Systematic direct observation (SDO) is the most commonly used progress monitoring tool used in published examples of FBAs and related interventions. SDO is the gold standard for progress monitoring of any behavior because, in addition to being highly reliable and valid when used by trained professionals, it is also a low inference and short latency measure of behavior (Christ, Riley-Tillman, & Chafouleas, 2009). It is low inference because it directly measures the behavior of interest, as opposed to rating scales that require people to rate discrete behaviors from which broad categories of behavior are deduced (e.g., anxiety, conduct problems). SDO is a short latency measure because the measurement occurs at the moment that the behavior occurs (i.e., there is almost no latency between behavior and measurement).

It is important to note the distinction between systematic and nonsystematic methods of direct observation. Nonsystematic methods are very common in schools and are often summarized in narrative form. SDO methods, by contrast, involve operational definitions, predefined observation periods, and coding systems (e.g., time sampling, continuous recording). To compare data over time, the systematic element is critical.

Direct behavior ratings (DBRs) have recently emerged as an alternative or supplement to SDO for progress monitoring of behavior. DBRs have appeared in the literature under the names *daily behavior report cards, school– home notes,* and *daily progress reports* (Chafouleas, Riley-Tillman, & Christ, 2009). A recent series of studies indicates that they can be useful tools for progress monitoring of behavior under certain conditions, which will be addressed later in this chapter. Here, we review these two methods of progress monitoring for FBA-based behavior intervention plans.

Systematic Direct Observation

SDO is a process in which behavior is observed and measured using precisely defined behaviors and some dimension of the behavior, such as frequency,

Functional Behavioral Assessment

duration, latency, or intensity (Salvia & Ysseldyke, 2001). One of the defining features of SDO, as compared to nonsystematic direct observation, is that it involves measurement—meaning that behaviors are converted into numbers. The numbers can then be used to compare progress over time in a meaningful way.

The strengths of SDO as a tool for progress monitoring, in addition to being a low-inference and short-latency measure, include its validity, reliability, and repeatability. A measure is valid to the degree that it measures what it claims to measure. It is difficult to imagine a more valid way to measure something than to directly observe it. In essence, directly observing behavior is the behavioral equivalent to the astronomer's process of measuring stars based on what is seen through a telescope. It is difficult to discredit astronomical observations through a telescope just as it is difficult to discredit direct observation of behavior. Another strength of SDO is its reliability. Although reliability measures of SDO are generally high, the reliability of SDO is not inherent in the measure but rather depends on a number of factors, including the training of the observers, the precision with which the behavior is defined, and the ease with which the observation system can be used. Therefore, to ensure the reliability of SDO, the user must create a clear and precise definition of the behavior, so that any two people who see it can agree that the observed behavior fits the definition. After the behavior is precisely defined, then the observational tool must be developed to be as simple as possible. For example, recording ten different behaviors every 5 seconds is more difficult to do well than recording one behavior every 10 seconds. Finally, observers must be trained to use the definition and the system before using their data. Methods for calculating reliability based on the observations of two different observers for the same period have been articulated in the literature (see Cooper, Heron, & Heward, 2007; Hartmann, 1977), but generally involve calculating a correlation between two scores. A final strength of SDO is its repeatability. There is no reason why the same observation system could not be used over and over again without negatively impacting the results.

Although SDO has clear strengths as a progress monitoring measure in FBAs and related interventions, it has two limitations that should be considered. First, SDO is labor intensive. It requires that the person conducting the SDO do nothing but observe for a set period of time (e.g., 30 minutes) on a regular basis. When all of these observations are added together, it can take many hours of professional time to adequately document behavioral progress over time. SDO is also limited in that it often leads to reactivity. *Reactivity* refers to that behavior exhibited by the person being observed in reaction to the observation itself. In other words, reactivity is the unusual behavior that results from knowing that one is being watched. It can take several sessions before reactivity diminishes, and each session in which the observer is merely waiting for behavior to become "typical" adds to the labor intensity of the process.

Direct Observation Progress Monitoring System

Many different forms and systems can be used reliably and validly when conducting SDO. In an effort to create a uniform process for readers of this book, we have developed the *Direct Observation Progress Monitoring System* (DOPMS; Figure 4.1). The DOPMS uses a momentary time sampling procedure, wherein behavior is recorded only during brief moments throughout the observation period. This method is used because momentary time sampling has been demonstrated to be the most accurate estimate of actual behavior, as compared to other methods such as partial-interval time sampling and whole-interval time sampling (Saudargas & Zanolli, 1990). And, it involves less effort by the observer since it only requires the observer to observe briefly (approximately 1 second) every so often (e.g., every 10 seconds, in the case of the DOPMS).

Basic Information

When using the DOPMS, the observer begins by recording basic information about the observation period, such as the name of the person being observed, the date, and the start and stop time. The start and stop time should be 20 minutes apart, as the DOPMS is designed for 20-minute observation periods. To be able to compare data over time, it is important to always observe during the same time and in the same location. Observers should select a time and place when teachers report that the behavior in question is most frequent. Also included in this section of the form is a place to indicate whether this observation is for the baseline or intervention phase. This ensures that the different phases of progress monitoring can be clearly tracked. In some cases, a return to baseline may occur, or a different intervention may be implemented. In these cases, the option exists to indicate "other" and then describe the condition. During the FBA phase of progress monitoring in Tiers 2 and 3, it is recommended that teams collect at least three different observations before beginning intervention and label these observations as "baseline." It is acceptable to conduct more than three baseline

Direct Observation Progress Monitoring System

Person being observed: _____
Observer: _____
Date: _____ Start Time: _____ End Time: _____ Location: _____
Condition (circle one):   Baseline - Intervention - Other (describe):
PRECISE DEFINITION OF TARGET BEHAVIOR:
_____
_____
_____

Momentary Time Sampling

Directions: Using a stopwatch to keep time, observe for one-second at the specified time intervals (e.g., look for one second right away, record the behavior, then look again for one second at the 10-second mark, record the behavior, etc.). Record occurrence of behavior with an X and non-occurrence with an O.

Minute	:00 – :01	:10 – :11	:20 – :21	:30 – :31	:40 – :41	:50 – :51
0						
1						
2						
3						
4						
5						
6						
7						
8						
9						
10						
11						
12						
13						
14						
15						
16						
17						
18						
19						

INFORMAL NOTES:_____

SUMMARY

of Intervals with target behavior: _____ / 120 = _____% of intervals with target behavior

FIGURE 4.1 Direct Observation Progress Monitoring System.

observations, but it is preferable to begin the intervention phase reasonably soon, given the findings from the FBA and the complexity of the plan that results from the FBA. We recommend that observations occur at least once or twice per week. More often is acceptable but requires more time commitment in a week than is typically available for working with one student.

Precise Definition

The next section of the DOPMS includes a space to write a precise definition of the target behavior. It is important to use the same definition throughout the entire course of working with a student. The precise definition of the behavior used here will be the same precise definition of the behavior used for all elements of the FBA and related intervention. For example, when conducting FBA observations and interviews in Tier 3 (see Chapter 6), the definition of the behavior created for the DOPMS will be used for consistency across measures. The development of a precise definition of target behavior begins by answering the question "What does the behavior look like?" For example, we may be working with a student whose teacher describes her as defiant and disruptive, but what does this look like? Defiance could mean that the student uses inappropriate words directed at the teacher, or it could mean that the student refuses to comply with commands. Disruptive could mean any number of possible things including yelling, being out of seat, poking peers, or making noises with a pencil. A good, precise definition is one that leads to agreement between multiple observers regarding whether or not the behavior has occurred during an observation. So, a *poor* precise definition would be "disruptive." A *better* precise definition would be "yelling." But this could still be improved because not all observers may agree on the difference between yelling and talking. So, the *best* precise definition, in this case, would be "using words or vocal noises at a level that can be heard more than 10 feet away when not in response to being asked a question by a teacher." This definition includes sufficient detail so that it is unlikely that any instance of the target behavior would be overlooked or that any non-instance of the target behavior would be incorrectly recorded as an instance of the behavior. (A tip when developing precise definitions is to think of examples of behavior that would look similar to the target behavior but shouldn't be included and then write the definition so that it avoids including those examples, while including every relevant feature of the targeted behavior.)

The precise definition of the target behavior is included on the DOPMS form to remind the observer of what is being observed. It is easy to drift away from using this definition if it is not reviewed on a regular basis. The process of rewriting it each time that an observation occurs should serve to reduce this observer drift.

Behavior Recording

The next section of the DOPMS is the behavior recording section. This is arranged as a 10-second momentary time sample conducted over a 20-minute observation period. To keep track of the 10-second intervals, observers should have a stopwatch. The observations will be very brief—just 1 second at a time.

At the end of the predetermined second, the observer records the occurrence or nonoccurrence of the target behavior using an "X" for occurrence and an "O" for nonoccurrence. The observer then waits until the next specified observation interval and then records whether the target behavior occurred or did not occur during that 1-second interval. The observations occur at the 0- to 1-second mark, 10- to 11-second mark, 20- to 21-second mark, 30- to 31-second mark, 40- to 41-second mark, and the 50- to 51-second mark each minute. Any behavior that occurs at times other than those 1-second observation intervals is ignored by the observer and not recorded. Brief directions for recording behavior are included on the form.

Several precautions should be considered to reduce reactivity during behavior recording. First, it is recommended that the observer position her- or himself in the observation setting in such a way as to be as nonintrusive as possible. In classrooms, back corners are good as long as the student can still be observed clearly. Observers should not be positioned in front of the child in an obvious manner. Second, the observer should avoid focusing all attention on one student. The observer should scan the room regularly and minimize the appearance of observing one particular student. If students ask who is being observed, it is best to respond in a way that does not directly answer the question (e.g., "I watch a lot of students as part of my job.")

Near the bottom of the form is a place to write informal notes. Informal notes could include things like unusual occurrences during the observation (e.g., substitute teacher in class), unusual features of behavior (e.g., yelling was much louder than on most days), or appearance of target student (e.g., student appeared tired). This information can be used to contextualize the data when unexpected patterns emerge over time.

Summary
The final section of the DOPMS is the summary section. In this section, the observer records the number of occurrences of the target behavior over the 20-minute observation period and then calculates a percentage of intervals with the target behavior by dividing that number by 120 (e.g., 40 occurrences/ 120 intervals = 33.3% of intervals with target behavior). The percent-of-intervals metric will then be used to compare observations over time.

Direct Behavior Ratings
DBRs combine the advantages of SDO and behavior rating scales as an efficient method of progress monitoring of behavior (Chafouleas et al., 2009).

SDO has been considered the gold standard in progress monitoring because of its inherent validity and repeatability. Behavior ratings scales, in comparison, offer a more efficient method of measuring behavior because they do not require significant time investment to complete. DBRs combine these advantages by being repeatable with minimal time investment.

DBRs have existed as a casual method of recording behavior in schools for a long time. It is only recently that they have been systematically evaluated for their practical and technical properties as a tool for progress monitoring of behavior (see Chafouleas et al., 2009). Their practical properties include efficiency, flexibility, and repeatability. The efficiency is based on the fact that they require no more than a minute of time for a rater to complete, and the raters are people who are already in the context in which behavior is evaluated (e.g., teacher, paraprofessional). The flexibility relates to the fact that they can be adapted to accommodate numerous behaviors and assessment contexts. They are repeatable because there is nothing about their use at one point in time that affects their use at a later point in time, regardless of the latency between ratings. The technical properties of DBRs include reliability, validity, and directness. DBR ratings are considered direct because behavior is rated very shortly after it is observed, typically at the end of a 15- to 60-minute observation period. Although this is not as direct as SDO, which involves rating behavior immediately as it occurs, it is considerably more direct than behavior rating scales that involve reporting on behavior that occurred up to several months ago. The validity of DBRs is largely related to the fact that the behavior rated is the behavior of interest, rather than a combination of many different specific behaviors combined to create an abstract category, as is the case with behavior ratings scales. Further, Riley-Tillman, Chafouleas, Sassu, Chanese, and Glazer (2008) found that DBRs correlated significantly with SDO data for the same behaviors observed by the same raters. The reliability of DBRs is affected by the same general factors that affect the reliability of SDO. For example, the amount of training that raters receive affects the agreement between raters who are observing during the same period (Schlientz, Riley-Tillman, Briesch, Walcott, & Chafouleas, 2009).

DBR Forms
Figures 4.2 and 4.3 are DBR forms that have been developed by Chafouleas, Riley-Tillman, Christ, and Sugai (2009) and are available on the website http://www.directbehaviorratings.com. The first form includes three standard behaviors, including academically engaged, respectful, and disruptive.

Direct Behavior Rating (DBR) Form: 3 Standard Behaviors

Date:	Student:	Activity Description:
M T W Th F	Rater:	

Observation Time:	Behavior Descriptions:
Start:_____ End:_____ _ Check if no observation today	**Academically engaged** is actively or passively participating in the classroom activity. For example: writing, raising hand, answering a question, talking about a lesson, listening to the teacher, reading silently, or looking at instructional materials. **Respectful** is defined as compliant and polite behavior in response to adult direction and/or interactions with peers and adults. For example: follows teacher direction, pro-social interaction with peers, positive response to adult request, verbal or physical disruption without a negative tone/connotation. **Disruptive** is student action that interrupts regular school or classroom activity. For example: out of seat, fidgeting, playing with objects, acting aggressively, talking/yelling about things that are unrelated to classroom instruction.

<u>Directions</u>: Place a mark along the line that best reflects <u>the percentage of total time</u> the student exhibited each target behavior. Note that the percentages do not need to total 100% across behaviors since some behaviors may occur.

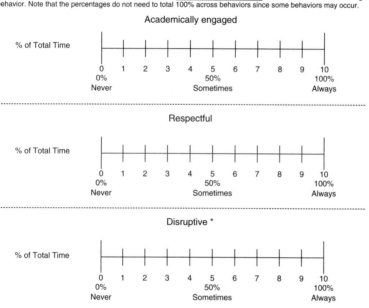

*Remember that a lower score for "Disruptive" is more desirable.

FIGURE 4.2 Direct Behavior Rating Form with standard behaviors included.

The definitions of these behaviors are provided on the form. One advantage to using this form is that the user can train all staff in a school to use the same behavior definitions for all students whose behavior is being monitored. Since training in the use of the form—including operational definitions

Direct Behavior Rating (DBR) Form – Fill-in Behaviors

Date:	Student:	Activity Description:
M T W Th F	Rater:	

Observation Time:
 	
Start:_____
 	
End:_____
 	
_ Check if no
   observation
   today
	Behavior Descriptions:	

Directions: Place a mark along the line that best reflects the percentage of total time the student exhibited each target behavior. Note that the percentages do not need to total 100% across behaviors since some behaviors may co-vary. If desired, an additional behavior may be defined and rated.

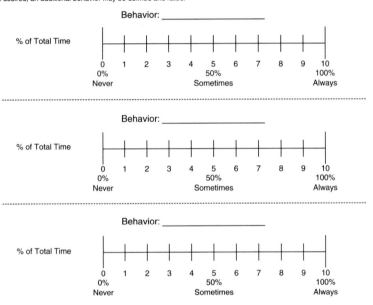

FIGURE 4.3 Direct Behavior Rating Form with space to fill in describing the behaviors.

of observed behaviors—affects reliability of the data, these standard behaviors can increase the quality of the data being collected. The second DBR form is the same as the first except that the behaviors are left blank. This allows for more specific behaviors to be observed. This form is appropriate when the team managing the progress monitoring process decides that it will

Functional Behavioral Assessment

be most useful to monitor the same behaviors as were measured during the FBA process, using the same definitions.

The directions for using these DBR forms are written on the forms. Beyond the easy-to-understand directions, we offer a few guidelines that will facilitate the gathering of useful information. First, it is recommended that the observations occur at the same time each day and last no longer than 60 minutes. Recent studies have indicated that estimates of behavior on DBR forms, especially estimations of problem behavior, are negatively affected by longer observation periods (Riley-Tillman, Christ, Chafouleas, Boise, & Briesch, 2010). Second, information should be recorded onto the form immediately after the observation period to ensure the most accurate scoring. If the observer (teacher) waits more than a few moments after the observation period to record data, the data will likely be affected by a broader time sample and memory errors. Third, it is important to review the definitions of behaviors before each observation period, so that the observer does not drift away from the original definitions over time. When observers drift over time to the use of nonstandard definitions of behavior, then the data collected early in the process (i.e., the first few days) are not directly comparable to data collected later in the process (i.e., the last few days). The effects are rather like using a ruler to measure something every day but letting the ruler warp and shrink over time. It could appear that the object observed has gotten shorter when in fact it has stayed the same size or grown. In the same way, observer drift can make behavior appear to increase or decrease when in reality it has stayed stable or changed in some other direction. More information about the use of these forms can be found at http://www.directbehaviorratings.com.

Decision-making Process

We have reviewed the data sources that are appropriate for progress monitoring of FBA-based interventions. For these data to be useful for decision making, they need to be summarized into a form that is easily understandable. Graphs have generally been found to be an efficient and understandable method of communicating progress monitoring data (Johnston & Pennypacker, 1993; Michael, 1974). Therefore, we will begin by reviewing the process of graphing behavior data and interpreting graphs.

Graphing Progress Monitoring Data

Although there are many different formats for graphs, the line graph is the most commonly used when working with behavior change over time

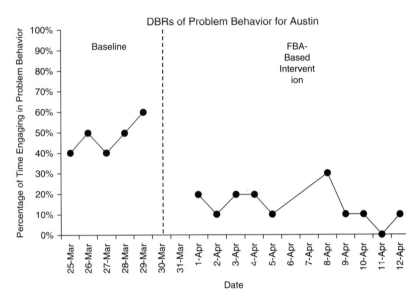

FIGURE 4.4 Progress monitoring line graph example.

(Cooper et al., 2007). Figure 4.4 illustrates a typical line graph with all of the critical components necessary for visual analysis. The critical components of a simple line graph for progress monitoring include the following (Cooper et al., 2007):

- The horizontal access (or x-axis) is used as a measure of the passage of time. In the example in Figure 4.4, dates are reported as the measure of time, but it is also acceptable to report time on the horizontal axis as sessions, trials, etc.
- The vertical access (or y-axis) indicates the value of the behavior measured. Figure 4.4 reports behavior using percentage of time that the target student, Austin, engaged in problem behavior as measured using DBRs. Other typical metrics for the vertical axis include frequency of behavior and percentage of intervals with observed behavior. Percentage of intervals would be the proper metric when using the DOPMS described in this chapter (e.g., 0%, 10%, 20%).
- A dashed line is used to indicate any change in conditions during progress monitoring. Figure 4.4 had only two conditions: baseline and FBA-based intervention. It is also

Functional Behavioral Assessment

reasonable to change the intervention or return to a baseline condition, in which case more condition-change lines would be used.

- Labels for conditions are written above the data in each condition. In Figure 4.4 the condition labels are "Baseline" and "FBA-Based Intervention."
- Data are plotted as points. Each point clarifies the amount of behavior observed and the time when the observation occurred. Figure 4.4 includes 3 weeks' worth of daily DBR data for 15 total data points.
- The path of the data over time is indicated with lines connecting the data points. When all of the other critical components are included in the graph, it should be very easy to visually recognize what is happening with the data based on the lines in the graph. In the example of Figure 4.4, it is clear that the behavior decreased after the FBA-based intervention was implemented.
- Each figure should have a caption that explains what the data shows as concisely as possible. The figure caption for Figure 4.4 is "DBRs of Problem Behavior for Austin," which explains what is measured (problem behavior), how it is measured (DBRs), and whose behavior is being reported (Austin's).

Technology can be used to develop graphs of progress monitoring data, but it is possible to create a fairly well-designed graph using a pencil/pen and graphing paper. If you choose to use technology, the authors have found Microsoft Excel to be a good and efficient option (the example from Figure 4.4 was created using Microsoft Excel). For more information on the use of Microsoft Excel in creating various line graphs, please see Dixon and colleagues' (2009) tutorial published in the *Journal of Applied Behavior Analysis*. The function-based behavior intervention plan document in Chapter 7 of this book includes a page with a blank line graph for teams to use for progress monitoring (see Figure 7.2). Examples for the use of this graph are also included in Chapter 7 (see Figure 7.3).

To restate an important point: Progress monitoring data is graphed to support good decision making. In other words, SDO and DBR data that have been collected are unlikely to affect decisions if they are left in raw form and never summarized on graphs. When making decisions based on graphed progress monitoring data, there are a few features of the data to attend to. Perhaps the most salient feature of the data line graph is the *level* of the data. In Figure 4.4 it is clear that the level of the problem behavior is higher during baseline than it is during FBA-based intervention. This observation alone would likely to lead to the decision that the intervention is working well and should be continued for the present. Another feature to consider is *stability*— the amount of change between data points over time. Low stability (e.g., high behavior one day, low behavior the next day, then high behavior again the next day) would imply that something important is affecting the behavior, other than the intervention, even if the level of the behavior went down during intervention. Therefore, some change in the intervention would be recommended to create more stability. Another feature of the data to consider would be *trend*—the direction in which the data points are moving over time. If the level of behavior is lower during intervention than during baseline, but the trend in the behavior is upward—meaning that the level is increasing over time—then a change in intervention will likely be necessary in the near future to prevent a return to baseline levels.

At this point, it should be clear that the graphed progress monitoring data for behavior inform decisions about whether to continue, change, or discontinue the intervention. They do not, however, inform specific decisions, such as what changes should be made to the intervention. The information for more specific changes should be based on the information gathered during FBA (e.g., antecedents and consequences). The specific process for developing interventions from FBAs will be covered in Chapter 5 in regards to Tier 2 and in Chapter 7 in regards to Tier 3. The general processes for deciding whether to continue, change, or discontinue interventions are described below.

Decision-making Based on Goals
One way to avoid arbitrary decision making is to make decisions based on preestablished goals. If, for example, a team working with a student in Tier 2 or Tier 3 decides that the short-term goal for intervention is that the student will use an appropriate replacement behavior more often than a problem behavior within 4 weeks, and that the long-term goal for intervention is a 75% reduction in problem behavior within 12 weeks, then we know when to make decisions and whether or not a goal has been met. Table 4.1 summarizes the types of decisions that would reasonably be made using

Table 4.1 Progress monitoring and decision matrix

		Goal Met?	
		Yes	**No**
TYPE OF GOAL	Short-Term	Intervention Decision = **Continue**	Intervention Decision = **Change***
	Long-Term	Intervention Decision = **Fade**	Intervention Decision = **Change***

*The decision to change is not absolute. The team should consider whether enough progress has been made toward the goal to warrant an extension on the timeframe for goals before investing in the process of changing intervention.

short- and long-term goals. In the case in which short-term goals have been met, it is reasonable to continue with the intervention, with the expectation that the long-term goal is attainable given the current level of progress. Once long-term goals have been met, it is reasonable to consider fading the intervention. This logic is a foundation of the three-tiered model and differs from a more traditional disability-focused model, in which students tend to continue to receive indefinitely interventions defined in individualized education plans (Shinn, 1986). In a three-tiered model, the intensity of intervention is designed to match the intensity of behavior (Sugai & Horner, 2002). So, when a student's behavior meets a long-term goal, it is assumed that enough progress has been made that a lower level of support should be sufficient to maintain lower levels of problem behavior. In the case of a student receiving Tier 2 intervention, the intervention can likely be slowly faded and then removed, such that the student's behavior is maintained sufficiently by Tier 1 interventions in the school. In the case of a student at Tier 3, the same logic holds true but it is reasonable to assume that a lower-intensity Tier 2 intervention, rather than a reduction all the way down to Tier 1 interventions, will be necessary to support the student's behavior for a while. This would then necessitate the development of a new set of Tier 2 goals.

Now that we understand how short- and long-term behavior goals can facilitate quality decision making, we will review how to develop these goals using progress-monitoring data (e.g., SDOs and/or DBRs). One general rule of thumb is to develop goals that are more ambitious than conservative. Fuchs, Fuchs, and Deno (1985) found that the ambitiousness of goals was significantly associated with outcomes, such that more ambitious goals led to better outcomes. Another rule of thumb is to write short-term goals as small changes that we expect to see as the student makes progress toward long-terms goals, and to write long-term goals that focus on clear measures of the problem behavior (Fuchs, 2002). In other words, long-term goals should always be written in relation to the problem behavior being measured (e.g., a 50% decrease in DBRs for inappropriate language), but short-term goals can use the same behavior measurements as long-term goals (e.g., a 25% decrease in DBRs for inappropriate language) and/or address more specific behaviors (e.g., will say "please" at least 10 times per day; will not swear more than three times per day). The advantage to using the same measurement system for both short- and long-term goals is that is requires only one source of information for both goals that can be read from the same graph.

When determining the appropriate levels for goals (e.g., "problem behavior occurs in less than 10% of observed intervals for SDO" vs. "problem behavior occurs in less than 25% of observed intervals using SDO"), there are two things to consider. The first consideration is the *normative level* of the observed behavior. The normative level can be obtained by observing peers in a similar environments and determining the average level of that behavior. The second consideration is the baseline level of the observed behavior. If the levels are extremely discrepant from peers, it may not be reasonable to expect that the target student's behavior will improve to the level of peers within a short period of time. Although no specific formula is offered for combining these two values (normative levels and baseline levels) into a short- or long-term goal, it is likely that reasonable goals can be established when these values are considered along with the recommendation for ambitious goal setting.

Summary

This chapter reviewed the sources of data that can be used for progress monitoring of behavior when FBA-based interventions are being developed and implemented. It also reviewed the process of making decisions based on progress monitoring data. SDOs and DBRs each have value in progress monitoring, and both can be graphed to facilitate decision making. Decision making is enhanced when decisions are based on short- and long-term goals, and these goals should be written to reference the progress monitoring data. In the next chapters, we will return to the primary focus of this book, which is the gathering of FBA data and the development of effective interventions based on that FBA data.

5

■■■

Tier 2 Functional Behavioral Assessment

As with all tiers, the *definition* of functional behavioral assessment (FBA) at Tier 2 is a process of identifying antecedents and consequences of problem behavior, the *outcome* of FBA at Tier 2 is the development of a precision hypothesis statement, and the *purpose* of FBA at Tier 2 is to develop effective interventions.

When conducting a Tier 2 FBA the population served is a *targeted group of students at-risk* who do not respond to Tier 1 interventions, the data collected are *brief interviews and review of existing records*, and the interventions used are *evidence-based package interventions*.

The importance of Tier 2 assessments and interventions has been a recent focus for educators. Researchers traditionally have focused their efforts on Tier 1 and Tier 3 processes, but only more recently has the focus expanded to Tier 2 (Todd, Campbell, Meyer, & Horner, 2008). FBAs at Tier 2 are one step closer to the traditional process with which school social workers are familiar because they focus on assessing the function of behavior for each student in a group separately. Fynaardt and Richardson (2010) note that the intensity of FBA should match the intensity of the problem behaviors, such that FBAs at Tier 2 are brief and based on record reviews and conversations with teachers. As noted in both Chapters 2 and 3, FBA is a process (not a specific procedure) of gathering information about setting events, antecedents, behaviors, and consequences that leads to a functional hypothesis and informs an intervention. Level of confidence in the hypothesis will improve at each tier, with the most confidence generated at Tier 3.

In aligning with the Response to Intervention (RtI) framework, FBAs at the Tier 2 targeted group level apply to students who have been identified as nonresponders to Tier 1 school-wide interventions based on the analysis of school-wide data, and they culminate in the use of individual student data to develop interventions and track outcomes.

The focus of this chapter is on how to utilize FBA as an efficient way to meet the behavioral needs of at-risk students. This chapter is unique in that it begins to explore the matching of package Tier 2 interventions to the function of behavior identified in the FBA process.

The Team Process of Tier 2 Functional Behavioral Assessments

As is the case with all tiers of FBA, Tier 2 of the FBA process is managed by a team. This team can be the same as that involved in Tier 1, or a separate team. Anderson and Scott (2009) recommend that the team from Tier 2 should be the same team that manages Tier 3 because these two tiers both require behavioral expertise in FBAs, someone who can allocate resources, and familiarity with general and special education in the school. If separate teams manage each tier, a clear avenue of communication must exist between them, so that information from assessments and interventions carries across and informs each tier. For this reason, it is most efficient to maintain the same team across tiers when possible.

The Tier 2 team will share responsibility for data collection and intervention planning. For example, although the school social worker may have the most advanced skills in organizing information and resources across numerous systems (e.g., home, school, special education, administration), other team members, such as a school psychologist, may also have advanced skills in required tasks, such as interviewing. The key to proper team functioning is to meet on a regular basis, divide responsibilities between meetings, and then meet as a whole group to discuss implications of data gathered between meetings. We recommend that the team meet at least every other week to ensure that student needs are addressed in a timely manner.

Transition from Tier 1 to Tier 2

In Chapter 3, we saw how students might be identified for Tier 2. In the middle school case (see Chapter 3) the team reviewed the Big Six discipline data and discovered that the problem with disrespect in the classroom is not school-wide; rather, it can be attributed to a subset of students who receive the most referrals for this issue. What is unique to a three-tiered prevention system is that students in need of more targeted FBA supports can be identified through the review of school-wide data. This differs from the more common practice of identifying students for additional support based solely on referrals from teachers, other school personnel, or student self-referrals. A common criteria applied when identifying students for Tier 2 FBA-based services using school-wide data is two to seven office discipline referrals (ODRs) per year (Fynaardt & Richardson 2010; Horner, Sugai, Todd, & Lewis-Palmer, 2005).

Data that will be preserved from the Tier 1 process into the Tier 2 FBA process will be those school-wide data that led the team to decide that an issue was attributable to a group of students, which includes the hypothesize function of the behavior. The data would then be disaggregated, and individual student data for the group of students are reviewed for the Tier 2 FBA.

Functional Behavioral Assessment Data Process at Tier 2

At Tier 2, FBA is the application of the functional model to a group of at-risk students that have behavior problems that impact their learning. To develop a precision hypothesis statement that helps a team match the function of the students' behavior to available evidence-based package interventions, the Tier 2 FBA data collection process will involve, for each student, review of ODR data, a review of other records, and a brief FBA teacher interview.

Review of Office Discipline Referral Data

It is important for team members to be aware of the results of the data analysis at Tier 1 that resulted in students being referred to Tier 2. These data include clear patterns of setting events/antecedents, behaviors, and consequences from ODRs. These data can be identified by summarizing all of an individual student's ODRs (see Figure 5.1). In the example in Figure 5.1, it appears that the problem behavior of this student is occurring in the morning, in the classroom, and is maintained by escaping (avoiding) tasks. As described in Chapter 3, it is only possible to make this degree of functional

Date	Grade	Staff	Time	Location	Problem Behavior	Motivation	Others Involved	Admin Decision
10/10/10	8	Hudson	9:35am	Class	Disrespect	Avoid task	None	Parent
10/04/10	8	Hudson	9:35am	Class	Disrespect	Avoid task	None	Loss priv
10/1/10	8	Hudson	9:45am	Class	Disrespect	Obtain peer attention	None	Parent
9/22/10	8	Hudson	10:00am	Class	Disrespect	Avoid task	None	Loss priv
9/14/10	8	Hudson	9:25am	Class	Disrespect	Avoid task	None	Conf

FIGURE 5.1 Example of summary of office discipline referral data for an individual student at Tier 2.

interpretation from ODR data when the school has invested in the process of making ODR data meaningful. Since the ODRs in the example are all coming from the same time frame in the classroom, it would be important to follow-up with the teacher during a later interview and ask what is occurring consistently in the classroom at this time (e.g., earth science, math, reading, independent work, group work) that would explain the setting event and antecedent conditions more clearly (i.e., what is happening at that time that the student is trying to avoid his problem behavior).

Brief Review of Other Records

The purpose of the record review is to examine existing data, such as attendance, grades, standardized tests, demographics (e.g., number of schools attended, number of home addresses), and visits to the school nurse. In a Tier 2 FBA, the review of the student's record is a quick analysis of the student's archival data that can inform interventions. When reviewing records, teams should remember that relevant information is not always evident. It is important for a team to be selective and purposeful about the information sought (Steege & Watson, 2009). Information should be reviewed for student strengths and for patterns that interfere with school success, such as high mobility between schools, frequent changes of address, series of excused or unexcused absences, grades, and health records, including visits to the school nurse. Any information that might indicate antecedents or functions of behavior and/or support preliminary hypotheses regarding the function of behavior will be important to present to the team. Figure 5.2 presents a form that a team could use when conducting a record review in a Tier 2 FBA.

Functional Behavioral Assessment

Brief Functional Behavioral Assessment Interview

The goal of collecting data at Tier 2 is to determine the setting events, antecedents, and consequences of a problem behavior. An interview is one of the most efficient methods of data collection for an FBA, although not always the most accurate. In Tier 3 FBAs, interviews are semi-structured, take about 30 minutes to complete, and are designed to provide the rigor necessary to inform individual intervention development. Tier 2 interviews, in contrast, are largely unstructured and should take about 5–10 minutes. They involve simply asking teachers about the setting events, antecedents, and consequences for the problem behavior. The interview is very informal and provides enough information to inform a tentative precision hypothesis statement that can be used when matching the function of student behavior to evidence-based package interventions.

The brief FBA interview should be conducted with those school personnel who might have the most information about the student. In elementary

STUDENT RECORDS REVIEW

Name of Student: _____ Grade _____

Attendance (e.g., excused and unexcused absences, number of schools attended)

Number of days absent:

PK____ K____ 1st ____ 2nd____ 3rd____ 4th ____ 5th ____ 6th ____ 7th ____

8th ____ 9th ____ 10th ____ 11th ____ 12th ____

  Strengths/Patterns:

Health (e.g., frequency of visits to school nurse, medical history, medications)
PK____ K____ 1st ____ 2nd____ 3rd____ 4th ____ 5th ____ 6th ____ 7th ____

8th ____ 9th ____ 10th ____ 11th ____ 12th ____

  Strengths/Patterns:

Academics (e.g., grades, standardized test scores)
  Strengths/Patterns:

Social/Emotional (e.g. current stressors, information about previous behavior problems)
  Strengths/Patterns:

FIGURE 5.2 Tier 2 functional behavioral assessment record review form.

Brief FBA Interview

Name of student: _____ Date _____

Name of Interviewer: _____ Name of Person Interviewed: _____

Antecedent

Behavior

Consequence

Setting Event (if possible)

Additional notes

Summary Statement

Setting Event/Antecedent	Behavior	Maintaining Consequence

FIGURE 5.3 Brief Tier 2 Functional Behavioral Assessment Interview.

school, it is likely that the classroom teacher would be interviewed. However, in middle/junior high or high school, the team will need to identify which teacher or staff member might provide the most information regarding the student's behavior. Figure 5.3 provides an outline for a brief FBA interview. The interview form is very simple and includes places to write notes about the functional information discussed in the interview. Note that, after the interview is completed, the interviewer is encouraged to summarize the results in the box at the end of the interview form.

Middle School Case Example

This case example continues the middle school case example included at the end of Chapter 3 and involves a suburban middle school with an enrollment of 750 students in grades 7 and 8. The team reviewed data at the end of the previous academic year to determine if the current Tier 1 interventions were effective or if additional supports were needed. Following that review it was noted that a subgroup of students fell outside the benchmark for ODRs, and thus other tiers of intervention needed to be considered. The case presented in this chapter follows the team's review of one student in this subgroup

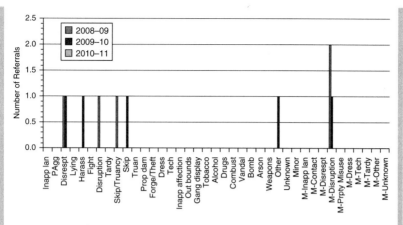

FIGURE 5.4 Individual student example for a graph of referrals by problem behavior.

identified at Tier 1. The same process would be replicated for each student being considered for Tier 2 FBA-based services.

Jessica is an eighth-grade student. Figure 5.4 shows the behaviors for which she received discipline referrals in her elementary school at grade 6 (2008–2009) and during her seventh grade year (2009–2010) at the middle school. Note that this example uses graphs for individual student data, as opposed to the tabular summaries of individual data from Figure 5.1 Since this example takes place at the beginning of the 2010–2011 school year, there are no data for the current year. However, these data will appear in the same format as they become available. Jessica has both minor and major ODRs, with a majority of her ODRs being categorized as verbal offenses (disrespect, harassment, and disruption).

The team next looks at the location in which the behaviors are occurring. It is clear in Figure 5.5 that most behavior prompting ODRs occurs in the classroom, closely followed by the hallway as a second source of referrals. There are no data available indicating the time of day the referrals have occurred. The team notes that this information would be useful in identifying environmental conditions that could contribute to behavior issues.

Next, the team reviewed the average number of ODRs per day per month (see Figure 5.6). Jessica had ODRs over five of the ten months in the 2008–2009 year and three of ten months in 2009–2010.

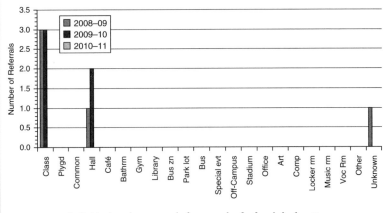

FIGURE 5.5 Individual student example for a graph of referrals by location.

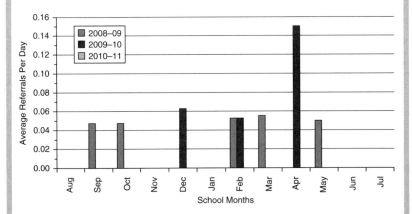

FIGURE 5.6 Individual student example for a graph of referrals per day per month.

There was no consistent pattern in the months in which she received and did not receive ODRs.

The team then looked at referrals by motivation (see Figure 5.7). In both years of data, the most frequently hypothesized function of the behavior was obtaining peer attention.

Following the examination of ODR data, the team identifies one team member, the school social worker, to take the lead in conducting a review of Jessica's educational records and a brief FBA interview. The school social worker reviews the records and notes that Jessica has a long history of attending school with few absences. It was not until seventh grade that she began skipping

Functional Behavioral Assessment

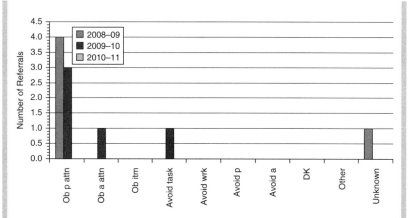

FIGURE 5.7 Individual student example for a graph of referrals by motivation.

STUDENT RECORDS REVIEW

Name of Student:__ **Jessica Smith** _____Grade____**8**_____

Attendance (e.g., excused and unexcused absences, number of schools attended)

Number of days absent:

PK ___ K **4** 1st **5** 2nd **6** 3rd **4** 4th **6** 5th **10** 6th **10** 7th **12**

8th ____ 9th ____ 10th ____ 11th ____ 12th ____

STRENGTHS/PATTERNS: **School records indicate that student attended the same elementary school K through 6th grade and has been at the same jr. high 7th and now 8th grade. Absences increased over time with a noticeable increase in 5th grade. Notes regarding absences during 7th grade indicated skipping classes to be an issue. Absences prior to 5th grade were within normal expectations for students.**

Health (e.g., frequency of visits to school nurse, medical history, medications)

PK ___ K **1** 1st **1** 2nd **2** 3rd **1** 4th **2** 5th **2** 6th **1**

7th **0** 8th ____ 9th ____ 10th ____ 11th ____ 12th ____

STRENGTHS/PATTERNS: **There is no pattern of school nurse visits beyond normal expectations for students. Records indicate that student is not taking medications at school and has no remarkable medical history that could impact behavior.**

Academics (e.g., grades, standardized test scores)

STRENGTHS/PATTERNS: **Student's grades were all A's and B's until 6th grade when student received C's in Math. In 7th grade student received C's in most classes and a D in Math. Student has a long history of good academic performance.**

Social/Emotional (e.g. current stressors, information about previous behavior problems)

STRENGTHS/PATTERNS: **Records indicate that the only evident life stressor is the move to a new address in the beginning of 7th grade. Student continues to live with both parents.**

FIGURE 5.8 Example of a completed Tier 2 record review for a middle school student.

class. Her grades also began to decline in seventh grade, especially in math. A recent stressor that could be contributing to the problem behavior is a move to a new home (see Figure 5.8).

A brief FBA interview was conducted with the homeroom teacher. Based on ODR information, the team recommended that this teacher would be able to provide the most accurate information possible for a brief FBA interview (see Figure 5.9). The results of the interview indicate that Jessica is verbally disruptive in class. In response to these disruptions, the class laughs at her and the teacher tries to redirect her to use more appropriate behavior. The information gathered in the brief interview and information from the ODR data and records review led the team to the development of a precision hypothesis statement. The process for developing a precision hypothesis statement is described in the next section.

Brief FBA Interview

Name of student:_ **Jessica Smith** _____ Date _ **October 15, 2010** _____
Name of Interviewer:_ **Michelle Alvarez** Name of Person Interviewed:_ **Mrs. Bell-Homeroom Teacher**

Antecedent

Class is responding to questions from the teacher

Behavior

Student yells out inappropriate answers and looks around room to see who is watching

Student makes comments "under her breath" about other students after they answer a question

Consequence

Peers laugh at student
Teacher asks student to answer question appropriately
Teacher asks student not to say anything unless she wants the whole class to hear
Teacher eventually sends student to office if behavior continues

Setting Event (if possible)

Additional notes

Summary Statement

Setting Event/Antecedent	Behavior	Maintaining Consequence
Group question responding	Verbal Disruptions	Peer attention (sent to office –escape?)

FIGURE 5.9 Middle School Case Brief Functional Behavioral Assessment Interview.

Precision Hypothesis Statement

In Chapter 3 the process of writing a precision hypothesis statement for Tier 1 was explained. A quick review reveals that a precision hypothesis statement is a precise definition of the problem that specifies setting events, antecedents, and consequences. An example provided was that, while the statement "too many referrals" (primary statement) may give you an idea of what the problem might be, the statement that "there were more ODRs for aggression in the cafeteria than last year," gives you more specific information. A precision hypothesis statement goes beyond the definition of the problem to include antecedents, such as time of day and location and a hypothesis about maintaining consequences. A precision hypothesis statement follows this general format:

> (*Fill in problem behavior*) is most likely to occur when (*Fill in antecedent*) occurs and is maintained by (*Fill in reinforcer*). This whole sequence is most likely when (*Fill in setting event*) occurs.

In Chapter 3, the precision hypothesis statement referred to all students, but in Tier 2, the statement describes the behavior of a specific student. Another difference in Tier 2 is that the precision hypothesis statement summarizes multiple sources of data that were collected in the Tier 2 FBA (ODRs, other archival records, and interview), whereas the Tier 1 precision hypothesis statement summarized only ODR data (or comparable school-wide data). Although there is no formula for how to integrate these sources of data, a good rule of thumb is to focus on which sources of data are most reliable and rely more heavily on those data when writing the hypothesis. The process of integrating multiple sources of data into a precision hypothesis statement is a more significant issue in Tier 3, and it is described in more detail in Chapter 6. For the middle school case example described above, the team developed the following precision hypothesis statement.

Precision Hypothesis Statement from Case Example

Based on interviews, ODR data, and records review, it appears that Jessica's verbal disruption is most likely to occur in the classroom, when students are answering teacher questions, and is maintained by obtaining peer attention. The setting events for Jessica's behavior are unclear at this point.

Tier 2 Interventions

At Tier 2, targeted interventions are delivered to individual students or groups of students. The interventions are not individualized but rather are research-based manualized or package programs delivered in a consistent manner across students. We utilize the broad term "package" program in this book to refer to research-based curriculums, programs, and interventions that have been developed to address student behaviors. We cannot emphasize enough the need to implement these programs with fidelity to increase the likelihood of good outcomes for students. Tier 2 interventions are cost-effective and efficient, and minimal assessment is required prior to implementation (Fairbanks, Sugai, Guardino, & Lathrop, 2007; March & Horner, 2002; McIntosh, Campbell, Carter, & Dickey, 2009). The importance of Tier 2 interventions cannot be overemphasized. When a student does not respond to a Tier 2 intervention, the team must determine if a modification to the intervention would improve outcomes, or if the intervention is not well matched to the student need. An incorrect answer at this decision point can lead to an unnecessary use of additional resources or a delay in providing needed supports for the students (McIntosh et al., 2009). Current research has indicated that if the function of the behavior is not addressed by the intervention, then positive outcomes for the student are less likely to occur (Ingram, Lewis-Palmer, & Sugai 2005; McIntosh et al., 2009). Therefore, it is important to match students referred for Tier 2 to interventions that address the function of behavior (Fynaardt & Richardson, 2010).

The reality of practice is that, at Tier 2, schools often assign students to existing group interventions—such as social skills groups—without considering the data (Campbell & Anderson, 2008) and the function of behavior (McIntosh et al., 2009). Before matching Tier 2 interventions to students' needs, the team must first evaluate interventions currently available in the school. Figure 5.10 provides some questions for the team to consider during this process.

Using the form from Figure 5.10, the team will explore the following questions for each of existing Tier 2 interventions:

- Is the intervention evidence-based?

The team will need to review the actual research that resulted in good outcomes for students. Research completed on package interventions is often

Evaluating Tier 2 Interventions in School

Intervention	Evaluation					
	Evidence-based?	Function addressed	Non-responder decision rule?	Implementation fidelity assessed?	Effective?	Decision
	Y / N	Attention Escape Both	Y / N	Y / N	Y / N	E M*
	Y / N	Attention Escape Both	Y / N	Y / N	Y / N	E M*
	Y / N	Attention Escape Both	Y / N	Y / N	Y / N	E M*
	Y / N	Attention Escape Both	Y / N	Y / N	Y / N	E M*

*E = eliminate; M = maintain

FIGURE 5.10 Form to guide the evaluation of Tier 2 interventions based on evidence and function. Adapted with permission from Positive Behavioral Interventions and Supports (PBIS) Training Manual (www.pbis.org).

available from the developer. There are several websites that provide a research synopsis and rating for package interventions in widespread use. These websites include the National Registry for Evidenced-based Programs and Practices (http://www.nrepp.samhsa.gov/), Blueprints for Violence Prevention (http://www.colorado.edu/cspv/blueprints/index.html), What Works Clearinghouse (http://ies.ed.gov/ncee/wwc/), and Collaborative for Academic, Social, and Emotional Learning (http://www.casel.org/database/index.php). As the team reviews curriculum and the research that supports it, they will need to decide whether there is enough research to demonstrate that this intervention has shown good outcomes for students similar to those that attend their school.

- What function is addressed by the intervention?

Although there are several functions of behavior, they can be placed into the two broad categories of obtaining something or escaping something.

The team will need to decide which function each of the interventions address. This can be accomplished by listing all of the program components and then listing next to them whether each addresses positive (attention) or negative (escape) reinforcement functions of behavior. It is important to have at least one package intervention available in the school for each broad function of behavior for the team to select to best meet the needs of students. Unfortunately, a gap appears to exist in the literature in terms of Tier 2 package interventions that address the escape function. Therefore, it is more likely that interventions reviewed will be more appropriate for attention-maintained behavior.

- Does the intervention provide a nonresponder decision rule? Or has the team identified a nonresponder decision rule?

In some cases, package interventions will provide the team with a nonresponder decision rule. The team must be able to answer the question, "At what point is the student not responding to this intervention?" This would lead to the modification of the current intervention, implementation of a different intervention, or the movement to the next tier of FBA-based support. In the absence of a nonresponder decision rule, the team will need to define the rule. For example, if the student's behavior does not clearly improve compared to baseline despite implementation of an intervention for 4 weeks, then the team can decide at that point that the student is not responding to the intervention.

- Does the intervention provide a tool to evaluate implementation fidelity?

The package intervention should provide a fidelity checklist that school personnel can complete as they are implementing the intervention. This allows the team to ensure that the intervention is implemented as it was designed, and its implementation does not contribute to the lack of response on the part of the student.

- Is the intervention effective based on local data?

When a school is using an intervention and deciding whether to continue its use, then that decision should be based largely on local evidence. The data collected on each student in the intervention should be combined to determine if it is effective in general. If one student out of five have experienced behavior reductions when in the intervention, or if no data have been collected on the outcomes of the intervention in the school, then answer to this question is "no."

- The team then makes a decision whether to maintain or eliminate the intervention.

The team decides whether to continue (maintain) to offer each package intervention or eliminate it from the list of Tier 2 options. Although there is no concrete rule to guide this decisions, it would generally be appropriate to maintain any interventions that have earned "yes" responses to every item and eliminate those with "no" responses to one or more items. It would also be recommended that the school maintain at least two package intervention options, one of which addresses the attention function and the other of which addresses the escape function.

These questions guide the team in selecting appropriate interventions from among package interventions currently available. Once the process is completed and interventions to address all functions of behavior are available, then behavior referrals can be made with a higher degree of confidence that there will be positive outcomes for students.

Intervention Planning and Progress Monitoring

When a Tier 2 FBA is completed and the school has identified its Tier 2 evidence-based package interventions, then students can be matched to the available interventions based on function. Since the interventions are prepackaged, there is no need to individualize plans for each student at Tier 2. Instead, priority should be placed on tracking each student receiving Tier 2 FBA-based interventions using one document. The Tier 2 FBA Tracking and Process Form (Figure 5.11) serves this purpose. This single-document, comprehensive tracking process is contrasted with the process in Tier 3, which involves writing individualized plans for each student and monitoring their progress using the individual plan. The Tier 2 Tracking and Process includes spaces to record basic information about the student (name, grade, homeroom teacher), when the brief FBA was completed, the hypothesized function of the behavior, the intervention selected, information about the timing of the intervention (begin and end date), and decisions about its continued use. For each student, there is room to record up to three different Tier 2 interventions for instances in which one or two interventions do not work and modifications are made or different interventions are selected.

Tier 2 FBA Tracking and Process Form

Students/ Grade/Homeroom Teacher	Date Brief FBA Competed	Hypothesized Function	Intervention Selected	Begin Date	End Date	Decision (different Tier 2 intervention, move to Tier 1, move to Tier 3)
1.						
2.						
3.						
4.						
5.						

FIGURE 5.11 Tier 2 functional behavioral tracking and process form.

The progress of each student receiving Tier 2 FBA-based interventions should be monitored using the processes described in Chapter 4 (e.g., regular data collection and graphing with direct behavior ratings and/or systematic direction observation). Decisions based on this data would be recorded on the Tier 2 FBA Tracking and Process Form (Figure 5.11). Since the team should have developed decision rules when reviewing interventions (see Figure 5.10), they will utilize these rules to determine whether students have responded to the intervention and can be moved back to Tier 1, or whether students have not responded and need to have the Tier 2 intervention modified or replaced by another Tier 2 intervention. If more than two Tier 2 interventions have been attempted (including modifications to the

Functional Behavioral Assessment

intervention), then the team may also need to consider a Tier 3 FBA process (described in Chapter 6).

Fairbanks, Sugai, Guardino, and Lathrop (2007) provide a good example of Tier 2 FBA-based intervention planning and decision making. They describe the cases of several students who were placed in the efficient and evidenced-based Tier 2 intervention Check In/Check Out (Crone, Horner, & Hawken, 2004) after brief FBAs indicated a good match for this intervention. Using graphs of systematic direct observation data (as described in Chapter 4), they demonstrate that several students responded well to the intervention, but several students did not. Those who did not respond received a more intense Tier 3 FBA process (as described in Chapter 6) and received individualized FBA-based intervention plans (as described in Chapter 7) that were effective in reducing problem behavior.

Tier 2 FBA-Based Intervention Planning and Monitoring
Fidelity Checklist

TASK	DATE COMPLETED
Step 1. Collect ODR data for an individual student and analyze them for a pattern of setting events, antecedents, behaviors, and consequences.	
Step 2. Conduct a review of archival records and a brief FBA interview with one staff member that is most knowledgeable about the student's behavior.	
Step 3. Analyze package interventions in school to determine which behavior function is addressed and if they are evidence-based.	
Step 4. Based on the ODR data, review of archival records, and brief FBA interview, the team develops a precision hypothesis statement for the individual student and matches the function of behavior to an existing evidence-based package intervention.	
Step 5. All students receiving Tier 2 FBA-based interventions are tracked on one document and their progress is monitored.	

Step 6. Each student's progress in Tier 2 is evaluated to determine if:
      Intervention should be maintained
      Intervention should be modified
      Tier 1 processes should be sufficient to support student's behavior needs
        -or-
      Tier 3 FBA will be necessary to support student's behavior needs	

FIGURE 5.12 Tier 2 Functional Behavioral Assessment Fidelity Checklist.

Summary

In Tier 2, the functional model is applied to students in need of supports beyond those available in Tier 1. A simple FBA is conducted at Tier 2 that includes a review of Tier 1 ODR data, a review of school records, and a brief FBA interview, after which the team matches the hypothesized function of the behavior to an existing evidence-based package intervention. The progress of the student is monitored, and if the student does not respond to the intervention, then the team will consider implementing another Tier 2 intervention or refer the student for a Tier 3 FBA. Figure 5.12 provides a fidelity checklist for the Tier 2 FBA process.

6

▪▪▪

Tier 3 Functional Behavioral Assessment

Tier 3 FBA encompasses what has traditionally been considered all of FBA. In other words, traditional research and training on FBA has focused almost exclusively on applications with individual students exhibiting significant behavior problems and has only recently been considered relevant for Tiers 1 and 2 in the prevention model. So, Tier 3 FBA is essentially "traditional" FBA because it focuses on applications with individual students who have significant behavior problems. Given that much has already been written about what we are referring to as "Tier 3" FBA in other sources, we will focus on only those elements that are critical for quality implementation. So far in this book, interventions based on FBAs have been covered within the same chapter as the assessment processes for each tier. Moving forward, the process of developing and implementing an effective Tier 3 intervention based on FBA will be covered separately in Chapter 7, as it is a broad topic with considerable material to cover. As with all tiers of prevention, the definition, outcomes, and purpose of FBA remain stable at Tier 3. The differences in FBA at Tier 3 are the data sources used, the intervention developed, and the population served.

As noted in Figure 2.3 in Chapter 2, Tier 3 FBA uses interviews and observations as primary sources of data, leads to the development of individualized BIPs, and is applied to individual students with significant behavior problems. The students who are served in Tier 3 will have arrived at this level of assessment and intervention through one of two routes: lack of response to interventions in Tiers 1 and 2 (persistence of the problem), or by demonstrating physically dangerous behavior (severity of the problem). It is generally expected that a student will have received assessment and intervention services from Tiers 1 and 2 before progressing to Tier 3 so as to increase

As with all tiers, the *definition* of functional behavioral assessment (FBA) at Tier 3 is a process of identifying antecedents and consequences of problem behavior, the *outcome* of FBA at Tier 3 is the development of a precision hypothesis statement, and the *purpose* of FBA at Tier 3 is to develop effective intervention.

When conducting a Tier 3 FBA, the population served is *individual students with severe and persistent problem behavior*, the data collected are *semi-structured interviews and systematic direct observations*, and the interventions developed are *individualized behavior intervention plans* (BIPs).

efficiency of services. However, exceptions should be made for those students whose behavior is too dangerous to risk delaying intense intervention. For example, if a student has only two office discipline referrals (ODRs), but the referrals included physical fighting early in the year and a weapons violation mid-year, then it would be prudent to begin the Tier 3 FBA process for this student to reduce the risk of harm to self and others. The students receiving Tier 3 FBAs are those who have demonstrated violent behavior or have exhibited less intense behavior problems that have been resistant to intervention.

The interviews and observations used in Tier 3 are formal and time-intensive. In contrast, the data sources used in Tiers 1 and 2 were adopted primarily for their efficiency. When dealing with the degree of behavior problem that defines Tier 3, it is no longer acceptable to abbreviate the data collection process in the manner used for Tier 1 and Tier 2 FBA, and the focus is instead on the quality of the data collected and the degree to which it leads to a high-degree of confidence in our precision hypothesis statement and effective individualized interventions. So, although brief FBA interviews were employed in Tier 2, the interviews in Tier 3 will be formally structured. Other sources of data that were gathered in Tiers 1 and 2 (e.g., ODR patterns for an individual student, brief FBA interviews) will also be reviewed in Tier 3 when developing precision hypothesis statements.

Indirect Sources of Data

In Tier 3, teams focus on high-quality data sources for the development of a precision hypothesis statement that informs intervention. These sources of data will be of two types—indirect data and direct data. Direct data, such as systematic direct observations, provide the highest degree of confidence for all of the reasons described in Chapter 4 (e.g., low inference, temporal proximity to the actual event). Indirect sources in Tier 3, such as semi-structured interviews with teachers and caregivers, provide a higher degree of confidence than was present in Tier 2's brief interviews and provide more qualitatively useful information that can be used when developing interventions. We begin by reviewing indirect sources of data used in Tier 3, with a focus on structured interviews.

Structured Interview

The only requirements for conducting FBA interviews are that the interview process results in the identification of antecedents, setting events, behavior, and consequences. The degree to which an interview is structured, however, will affect the confidence a team can have in its results. Structure ensures that key issues are not missed in the process, such as the range of potential specific variables that could function as antecedents or consequences for problem behavior. Structure in FBA interviews also ensures that the behavior described is not vague, but includes enough specificity as to be easily identified when it is observed (i.e., measurable) (Crone & Horner, 2003). Although several structured FBA interviews have been published (see Floyd, Phaneuf, & Wilckzynski, 2005; March et al., 2000; Steege & Watson, 2009), we will focus on the *Functional Assessment Checklist for Teachers and Staff* (FACTS; March et al., 2000) because it has been used in more than a dozen published, peer-reviewed research studies and has been demonstrated to have strong test–retest reliability, interobserver agreement, and convergent validity with direct observation and experimental functional analyses, as well as treatment utility and social validity (McIntosh et al., 2008). It also takes the technical terms of FBA (e.g., setting events, frequency of behavior) and translates them into more teacher-friendly language (e.g., predictors of behavior and how often behavior occurs). In short, it is a practical and psychometrically sound, semi-structured FBA interview, for use with teachers, that improves interventions (Filter & Horner, 2009).

Using the FACTS

The *FACTS* (March et al., 2000) is a two-part instrument shown in Figure 6.1. The first part, *FACTS-Part A*, is one page in length and provides an overview of the target student's behavior. The second part, *FACTS-Part B*, is also one page in length and is used to identify the functional antecedents, setting events, and consequences for one routine in which significant behavior has been reported. If the behavior occurs at a significant level across multiple routines (e.g., reading, math, and recess), then the interviewer may choose to use a separate Part B for each of those routines. So, each interview will involve only one Part A but could involve several Part Bs.

Before completing the FACTS-Part A, step 1 and part of step 4 should be completed (steps are labeled on the left side of the interview form). Step 1 includes information about the respondent, the interviewer, the name of the target student, and the date of the interview. Step 4 is a review of the routines in the student's typical schedule. For elementary students, these generally include different subjects and/or activities throughout the day such as group reading, social studies, math time, and art. For middle school and/or high

Functional Assessment Checklist for Teachers and Staff (FACTS-Part A)

Step 1 Student/Grade: _____   Date: _____
Interviewer: _____   Respondent(s): _____

Step 2 **Student Profile:** Please identify at least three strengths or contributions the student brings to school.
_____
_____

Step 3 **Problem Behavior(s): Identify problem behaviors**

___ Tardy	___ Fight/physical Aggression	___ Disruptive	___ Theft
___ Unresponsive	___ Inappropriate Language	___ Insubordination	___ Vandalism
___ Withdrawn	___ Verbal Harassment	___ Work not done	___ Other _____
	___ Verbally Inappropriate	___ Self-injury	
Describe problem behavior: _____			

Step 4 **Identifying Routines: Where, When and With Whom Problem Behaviors are Most Likely.**

Schedule (Times)	Activity	Likelihood of Problem Behavior						Specific Problem Behavior
		Low					High	
		1	2	3	4	5	6	
		1	2	3	4	5	6	
		1	2	3	4	5	6	
		1	2	3	4	5	6	
		1	2	3	4	5	6	
		1	2	3	4	5	6	
		1	2	3	4	5	6	
		1	2	3	4	5	6	
		1	2	3	4	5	6	
		1	2	3	4	5	6	
		1	2	3	4	5	6	

Step 5 **Select 1–3 Routines for further assessment: Select routines based on (a) similarity of activities (conditions) with ratings of 4, 5 or 6 and (b) similarity of problem behavior(s). Complete the FACTS-Part B for each routine identified.**

FIGURE 6.1 Functional Checklist for Teachers and Staff (FACTS)
Source: March, Horner, Lewis-Palmer, Brown, Crone, Todd & Carr (2000).

Functional Assessment Checklist for Teachers & Staff (FACTS-Part B)

Step 1   Student/Grade: _____   Date: _____
          Interviewer: _____   Respondent(s): _____

Step 2   **Routine/Activities/Context:** Which routine (only one) from the FACTS-Part A is assessed?

Routine/Activities/Context:	Problem Behavior(s)

Step 3   **Provide more detail about the problem behavior(s):**

What does the problem behavior(s) look like?

How often does the problem behavior(s) occur?

How long does the problem behavior(s) last when it does occur?

What is the intensity/level of danger of the problem behavior(s)?

Step 4   **What are the events that predict when the problem behavior(s) will occur? (Predictors)**

Related Issues (setting events)		Environmental Features	
___ illness	Other: _____	___ reprimand/correction	___ structured activity
___ drug use	_____	___ physical demands	___ unstructured time
___ negative social	_____	___ socially isolated	___ tasks too boring
___ conflict at home	_____	___ with peers	___ activity too long
___ academic failure	_____	___ Other	___ tasks too difficult

Step 5   **What consequences appear most likely to maintain the problem behavior(s)?**

Things that are Obtained		Things Avoided or Escaped From	
___ adult attention	Other: _____	___ hard tasks	Other: _____
___ peer attention	_____	___ reprimands	_____
___ preferred activity	_____	___ peer negatives	_____
___ money/things	_____	___ physical effort	_____
		___ adult attention	_____

SUMMARY OF BEHAVIOR
Identify the summary that will be used to build a plan of behavior support.

Step 6

Setting Events & Predictors	Problem Behavior(s)	Maintaining Consequence(s)

How confident are you that the <u>Summary of Behavior</u> is accurate?

Step 7

Not very confident					Very Confident
1	2	3	4	5	6

What current efforts have been used to control the problem behavior?

Step 8

Strategies for preventing problem behavior		Strategies for responding to problem behavior	
___ schedule change	Other: _____	___ reprimand	Other: _____
___ seating change	_____	___ office referral	_____
___ curriculum change	_____	___ detention	_____

FIGURE 6.1 Continued.

school, it is likely that each teacher being interviewed will have experience with only one subject during the day, in which case the routines may be broken down to include routines such as teacher-directed activities, independent seatwork, group work, and transitions. It is recommended that the routines themselves be written in the left columns of step 4 before meeting with the teacher or staff person, to avoid slowing down the interview by asking for this information during the interview. This can be accomplished by either asking the respondent for the information in advance of the interview or by reviewing the typical classroom schedule.

The interview begins in step 2 with a brief discussion of the student's strengths. This reminds the respondent and the interviewer that the student has positive attributes or behaviors rather than focusing exclusively on negative behavior. This information can also be considered when developing interventions as potential reinforcers or alternative behaviors.

In step 3, the respondent is asked to describe the target student's problem behaviors. A list of behaviors is included to ensure that behaviors are not overlooked simply because they were not immediately recalled by the respondent.

Step 4 of Part A is the routine analysis. After the activities and times of day have been filled in, preferably before the interview, the interviewer will go through each activity with the respondent, one at a time, to determine the likelihood of problem behavior and which behavior(s) occurs during the activity. This can be helpful because, when asked as an open-ended question such as, "When does problem behavior occur?," teachers and staff may provide vague responses such as, "All of the time." By considering each activity separately and rating behavior likelihood on a scale of 1 to 6, it is more likely that differences will emerge as to when the behavior occurs.

In step 5 of part A, the interviewer reviews the results from part 4 and selects for further discussion those routines/activities that had the highest likelihood of problem behavior. For each routine selected, a separate FACTS-Part B will be completed.

For the FACTS-Part B, step 1 uses the same information from step 1 of part A (general information), and step 2 provides a place to describe which routine and behavior is being reviewed. In step 3, significant detail is gathered about the primary problem behavior from this routine. If multiple problem behaviors are reported during this routine, then it is recommended that only the most significant behavior be discussed. The first question in step 3 allows the interviewer to develop and operationally define the problem behavior by describing what it actually looks like. This moves beyond the level of simply labeling a behavior and into the level of specificity necessary to measure the behavior. The respondent is then asked to approximate the frequency, duration, and intensity of the problem behavior using teacher-friendly language.

Step 4 in Part B focuses on antecedents and setting events, using lists of common antecedents and setting events. As noted in Chapter 2, setting events can be difficult to identify because they typically occur long before the behavior occurs, making the connection between the two unclear. Borgmeier (2003) found that reports of setting events had lower test–retest reliability estimates (0.62) than reports of antecedents (0.77) or consequences (0.92). Therefore, it is appropriate to ask respondents about variables that they believe may serve as setting events, but it is not necessary to struggle through it in order to identify a setting event. It is important to note, though, that sources of data in Tier 3 other than interviews (e.g., observations) are unlikely to identify setting events. Therefore, this is the best opportunity to sort setting events out for inclusion in a precision hypothesis statement. Antecedents (referred to as "predictors" on the FACTS) should not be as difficult to identify. Further, because it will be difficult to develop a quality FBA-based BIP if no antecedent is identified, the interviewer should work with the respondent to ensure confidence in the functional antecedent. Although not explicit in this form, it is recommended that the antecedent be identified with as much specificity as possible. For example, if the respondent reports that the antecedent is "tasks that are too difficult," it is important to determine which tasks are difficult (e.g., reading aloud vs. reading silently, multiplication vs. division). Or, if the antecedent is "with peers," then the interviewer should determine if there are specific peers that seem most important in predicting the behavior.

In step 5 of Part B, the interviewer asks about the maintaining consequences for the problem behavior. The consequences are divided into positive and negative reinforcers but described in teacher-friendly terminology: "Things that are obtained," and "Things that are avoided or escaped from." As with all checklist items in the FACTS, there is a space to include other responses with descriptions. It is recommended that the interviewer record as much specificity about the features of the reinforcer as possible. For example, if the reinforcer is "preferred activity," then the respondent should be asked what activities the target student prefers.

Step 6 of Part B is the summary statement, which is a cursory version of a precision hypothesis statement. The interviewer summarizes the findings of the interview in terms of setting events/antecedents (these two are combined on the form), behavior, and consequences. This step is tied to part 7 of the FACTS-Part B, during which the interviewer reads the summary statement from part 6 to the respondent and asks the respondent to rate her or his confidence that the summary statement accurately reflects what she or he observed of the student's behavior on a scale of 1 to 6, with 6 being the highest level of confidence. March et al. (2000) report that the following variables are likely to affect confidence ratings: "(a) how often the problem behavior occurs, (b) how long you have known the focus person, (c) how consistent the problem behaviors are, (d) if multiple functions are identified, and (e) if multiple behaviors occur together" (p. 5). As a rule of thumb, a high confidence rating suggests that the information will be valuable for intervention planning, and a low confidence rating suggests that more information will need to be gathered before planning intervention. Low confidence ratings can sometimes be increased by asking the respondent which aspect of the summary statement seems inaccurate and then discussing what a better description would be. The summary statement in part 6 can be changed accordingly.

Finally, in step 8 of Part B, the respondent describes strategies that have already been attempted by the respondent to improve behavior. These include both antecedent and consequence strategies. This information will be useful in that it represents interventions that are either unlikely to work (when building an FBA-based BIP) or that have not been implemented with fidelity, given that the behavior continues to occur at problematic levels.

Who to Interview and When
The FACTS is designed to be used with professionals in the school setting who have direct experience with the student's behavior. Borgmeier (2003) found that the amount of direct experience that a respondent has with a student's behavior and the respondent's self-rated level of knowledge of behavior theory predicted accurate reports of antecedents, setting events, behaviors, and consequences. Therefore, it is important to talk to people who have the most direct experience with the student's behavior, and to target those who have some experience with behavior theory.

As a general rule of thumb, it is important to interview multiple sources. Within the school, it is recommended that at least two or three professionals be interviewed. Additional information can be gathered by interviewing the target student and a parent or legal guardian. We have not included semi-structured FBA interviews for students or parents in this book, and it is acceptable to use the unstructured interview format (described in Chapter 5) with parents and students. This information will be used to supplement information gathered from school professionals using the FACTS, which will serve as the primary basis for school-based intervention planning. The decision to conduct student interviews should be based on the developmental level of the student. Lower elementary school-aged students generally are not reliable reporters of their own behavior, but high school students certainly can contribute their perspective on why their behavior is occurring. One example of a student FBA interview is the *Student-Guided Functional Assessment Interview* and can be found in O'Neill et al. (1997). Regardless of the format used, it is important that each interview end with a summary statement describing the perceived setting events, antecedents, behaviors, and consequences.

We recommend that interviews be the first source of information gathered during Tier 3 FBA. By doing so, the team will have a better sense of when the observations should occur and what to look for during observations. For example, the interview process should lead to an operational definition of a problem behavior. This operationally defined behavior will then be observed later in the process, at a time of day that the respondent indicated the problem behavior is most likely to occur.

Functional Behavioral Assessment Observation

The most direct method of collecting FBA information is direct observation. Systematic direct observation (SDO) was reviewed as a system for progress monitoring in Chapter 4 (with a focus on the Direct Observation Progress Monitoring System [DOPMS]), but here we review SDO as a system for gathering functional information about antecedents, behaviors, and consequences. As with any method of collecting FBA information, the only requirement is that information gathered include antecedents, behaviors, and consequences. Therefore, an informal (or nonsystematic) method—such as recording information on a blank piece of paper when a behavior occurs—is an option for direct observation in an FBA. However, this nonsystematic approach is more difficult to summarize for a precision hypothesis statement, and observers may overlook detail in describing the stimuli and behavior. Therefore, at Tier 3, when it is important to gather the highest quality information for individual behavior intervention planning, we recommend a systematic approach to direct observation and that observation be conducted by a trained professional during dedicated observation times.

Systematic Direct Observation

O'Neill and colleagues (1997) published the *Functional Assessment Observation Form* (FAOF), an SDO form for FBA. I (KJF) have used this form many times, and I've adapted it for this book with permission from O'Neill and colleagues and named it the *FBA Observation and Summary Form* (FBA-OSF). The FBA-OSF is a two-page form that includes a page to record up to 15 observed behavior incidents and a page to summarize the results of the observations to inform the development of a precision hypothesis statement (Figure 6.2).

Using the FBA-OSF

As with any FBA form, it is important to begin by recording the basic information, such as the target student's name and the name of the observer. Spaces are provided near the top of the FBA-OSF for this information.

The FBA-OSF is completed by placing an "x" in each box that describes the behavior observed, the details of the antecedent conditions, the perceived consequences, the location, and the date/time of the incident. Each row

FBA OBSERVATION AND SUMMARY FORM (FBA-OSF)

STUDENT: _____   OBSERVER: _____

BEHAVIOR INCIDENT #	BEHAVIORS (WRITE IN)			ANTECEDENTS — TASK LEVEL			ANTECEDENTS — CLASS ACTIVITY			ANTECEDENTS — INTERACTION		ALONE/NO ATTENTION	CONSEQUENCES — OBTAIN				CONSEQUENCES — AVOID/ESCAPE				CLASS/LOCATION (WRITE IN)		DATE/TIME		
				DIFFICULT	EASY	LONG	SEATWORK	TEACHER-LED INSTRUCTION	UNSTRUCTURED TIME	WITH ADULT	WITH PEER(S)		ADULT ATTENTION	PEER ATTENTION	TASK/ACTIVITY	TANGIBLE	ADULT ATTENTION	PEER ATTENTION	TASK/ACTIVITY	TANGIBLE			DATE:	DATE:	DATE:
1																									
2																									
3																									
4																									
5																									
6																									
7																									
8																									
9																									
10																									
11																									
12																									
13																									
14																									
15																									
TOTAL																									

Directions: For each behavior incident, place an X in the appropriate boxes across the corresponding row to indicate which behaviors, antecedents, and consequences were observed. After all observations are completed, create a summary statements that describes the antecedents and consequences that are most closely related to each behavior and build an intervention plan using this summary. A template for writing summary statements can be found on page 2 of this form.
Adapted with permission from the Functional Assessment Observation Form (O'Neill, Horner, Albin, Sprague, Storey, & Newton, 1997).

FIGURE 6.2 Functional Behavioral Assessment Observation and Summary Form (FBA-OSF).

SUMMARY STATEMENTS FROM FBA OBSERVATION

RESPONSE CLASS #1

ANTECEDENT	BEHAVIOR	CONSEQUENCE

RESPONSE CLASS #2

ANTECEDENT	BEHAVIOR	CONSEQUENCE

RESPONSE CLASS #3

ANTECEDENT	BEHAVIOR	CONSEQUENCE

Directions: For each behavior incident, place an X in the appropriate boxes across the corresponding row to indicate which behaviors, antecedents, and consequences were observed. After all observations are completed, create a summary statements that describes the antecedents and consequences that are most closely related to each behavior and build an intervention plan using this summary. A template for writing summary statements can be found on page 2 of this form.
Adapted with permission from the Functional Assessment Observation Form (O'Neill, Horner, Albin, Sprague, Storey, & Newton, 1997).

FIGURE 6.2 Continued.

represents a separate behavior incident, so that, when the first behavior occurs, all of the information from row 1 is completed. The 15 rows correspond to 15 different behavior incidents that can be recorded on one form. If more behaviors occur during the observations, a second copy of the FBA-OSF can be used to record incident 16 and beyond. The information about behaviors, antecedents, and consequences is provided in the columns across each row. As a general rule of thumb, it is acceptable to place an "x" in as many boxes as are appropriate given the observed behavior incident. For example, if the target student is engaging in (a) a difficult task (b) during independent seatwork (c) while receiving no attention, then it would be appropriate to place an "x" in each of the corresponding antecedent boxes.

The first thing to record on the FBA-OSF during a behavior incident is the observed behavior. The form contains four blank spaces to allow for the recording of four separate behaviors. Each behavior is written into the blank space. The observer should be able to write in at least one or two behaviors that were operationally defined during the interview phase of Tier 3. If other behaviors not described during the interview process occur, these behaviors can be added to the form as they are observed.

The next thing to record during a behavior incident is the perceived antecedents to the behavior. The FBA-OSF contains nine columns to describe the antecedents. The first subcategory of antecedent information is information about tasks. Difficult tasks, easy tasks, and long tasks have been identified as common antecedents to problem behavior (Filter, 2004; Newcomer & Lewis, 2004; Umbreit, Lane, & Dejud, 2004) and were therefore included as task subtypes. The next three subcategories of antecedents describe the general class activity (independent seatwork, teacher-led group instruction, or unstructured time). It is assumed that these three are mutually exclusive, so cannot occur at the same time. Another subcategory of antecedents describes interactions that were observed to occur. The interactions can be with the teacher and/or with peers. The last bit of information under antecedents is a column that is checked if the student is receiving no attention. A lack of attention is often, although not necessarily, a setting event for attention-maintained behaviors in that the lack of attention motivates the student to engage in behavior that draws attention to her- or himself.

After recording the behavior(s) and antecedents, the observer records the perceived consequences for the behavior incident. The consequences have been divided into positive reinforcers (labeled as "Obtain" on the form) and negative reinforcers (labeled as "Escape/Avoid" on the form) to match the general functional model described in Chapter 2. The categories of obtain and avoid are each subdivided into adult attention, peer attention, task/activity, and tangible (i.e., any item that can be physically manipulated). Another possible function of behavior, automatic reinforcement (i.e., non–socially mediated), has not been included on the form because it is not observable. However, automatic reinforcement can be deduced from a clear lack of any observable positive or negative reinforcement and included in precision hypothesis statements when appropriate. It is not always easy to determine the consequence for a behavior because not every behavior is reinforced every time it occurs and reinforcers are sometimes delayed. For example, a behavior can be maintained by obtaining adult attention even though it only leads to adult attention less than half of the time or several minutes after the behavior occurs. Therefore, it is important to use good professional judgment when recording observed consequences, and it is acceptable to not record a consequence if the consequence is unclear.

Other information in the FBA-OSF includes location of the incident and date/time of the incident. Location is likely to be classroom, hallway, cafeteria, library, playground, or other room (e.g., lab, gym) and is recorded in a blank space on the form. The location is likely to either remain constant or change only once or twice during the observation. This information can generally be filled out at the beginning of the observation, and new location information can be added when transitions to new locations occur during the observation. The date can be recorded in the columns provided and then the time can be written in the box under that column when a behavior incident occurs. So, the "Date/Time" column would be the only one on the form that does not use the "x" system when recording information. Rather, specific times for incidents are written under the column for the correct date.

The last row on the FBA-OSF is a place to tally all of the columns. We recommend that tallying occur only after at least 10 incidents have been observed across at least two observation periods. This should ensure that the observer is able to capture a pattern in the observed data before developing a precision hypothesis statement. These should be considered minimal criteria, and observing more than 10 incidents should further increase confidence in the data.

The second page of the FBA-OSF is a place to summarize the findings of observations in a simple antecedent-behavior-consequence (ABC) format. This is the information that will be combined with information from other data sources (e.g., FACTS interviews) to develop a precision hypothesis statement. The form includes space for three different ABC patterns under the labels, "Response Class #1, Response Class #2, and Response Class #3." A *response class* is a group of behaviors, each of which leads to the same consequence (Cooper, Heron, & Heward, 2007). In other words, a response class is actually defined by the function, not by behavior. So, each response class on page 2 should have only one consequence but could have multiple behaviors and/or antecedents. For example, Figure 6.3 illustrates two different response classes that were identified from the example FBA-OSF data. The first response class was "escape peer attention." There was only one behavior in this response class, and the antecedent was "seatwork with peers in math class." The second response class was "escape task/activity." There were two behaviors in this response class: "out-of-seat" and "inappropriate language," and the antecedent was "teacher-led instruction in reading class." Although screaming was once associated with the consequence of "obtain adult attention," and inappropriate language was once associated with the consequence of "escape adult attention," these were one-time occurrences and do not appear to constitute a pattern of behavior or separate response classes. Use of the FBA-OSF should result in at least one response summary. If no clear response class has emerged from the observations, then it is recommended that more observations be conducted until a pattern and response class is clear.

FBA OBSERVATION AND SUMMARY FORM (FBA-OSF)

STUDENT: **Aiden** OBSERVER: **Rachel**

BEHAVIOR INCIDENT #	Out-of-seat	screaming	Inappropriate language	TASK LEVEL — DIFFICULT	EASY	LONG	CLASS ACTIVITY — SEATWORK	TEACHER-LED INSTRUCTION	UNSTRUCTURED TIME	INTERACTION — WITH ADULT	WITH PEER(S)	ALONE/NO ATTENTION	OBTAIN — ADULT ATTENTION	PEER ATTENTION	TASK/ACTIVITY	TANGIBLE	AVOID/ESCAPE — ADULT ATTENTION	PEER ATTENTION	TASK/ACTIVITY	TANGIBLE	Math	Reading	DATE: Oct 3rd	DATE: Oct 5th	DATE:
1		X					X				X							X			X		9:30		
2	X	X					X				X							X			X		9:37		
3		X							X			X	X								X		9:58		
4		X					X				X							X			X		10:11		
5	X							X				X							X			X	1:15		
6			X					X				X							X			X	1:22		
7			X					X				X					X					X	1:30		
8		X					X				X							X			X			9:18	
9		X					X				X							X			X			9:21	
10		X					X				X							X			X			9:40	
11		X					X				X							X			X			9:45	
12			X					X				X							X			X		1:20	
13			X					X				X							X			X		1:23	
14	X		X					X				X							X			X		1:35	
15																									
TOTAL	3	8	5				7	6	1		7	7	1				1	7	5		8	6			

Directions: For each behavior incident, place an X in the appropriate boxes across the corresponding row to indicate which behaviors, antecedents, and consequences were observed. After all observations are completed, create a summary statements that describes the antecedents and consequences that are most closely related to each behavior and build an intervention plan using this summary. A template for writing summary statements can be found on page 2 of this form.
Adapted with permission from the Functional Assessment Observation Form (O'Neill, Horner, Albin, Sprague, Storey, & Newton, 1997).

SUMMARY STATEMENTS FROM FBA OBSERVATION: FBA-OSF (PAGE 2)

RESPONSE CLASS #1

ANTECEDENT	BEHAVIOR	CONSEQUENCE
Seatwork with peers in math class	**Screaming**	**Escape peer attention**

RESPONSE CLASS #2

ANTECEDENT	BEHAVIOR	CONSEQUENCE
Teacher led instruction in Reading class	**Out-of-seat & inappropriate language**	**Escape task/activity**

RESPONSE CLASS #3

ANTECEDENT	BEHAVIOR	CONSEQUENCE

Directions: For each behavior incident, place an X in the appropriate boxes across the corresponding row to indicate which behaviors, antecedents, and consequences were observed. After all observations are completed, create a summary statements that describes the antecedents and consequences that are most closely related to each behavior and build an intervention plan using this summary. A template for writing summary statements can be found on page 2 of this form.
Adapted with permission from the Functional Assessment Observation Form (O'Neill, Horner, Albin, Sprague, Storey, & Newton, 1997).

FIGURE 6.3 Example of a completed Functional Behavioral Assessment Observation and Summary Form (FBA-OSF).

Planning Observations: When, Where, and How

When planning FBA observations, it is recommended that the observations be scheduled at times and locations in which problem behaviors are most likely to occur. This information is gathered in step 4 the FACTS interview. Therefore, it is highly recommended that interviews occur before observations. Information from the interview will also include operational definitions of the behaviors that will be observed. By using these operational definitions during observation, the congruence between sources of data is increased. In other words, using the same definitions of behaviors during interviews and observations ensures that the information is consistent across data sources.

As with any observation, it is best to spend some time in the observation setting before collecting data, in order for the target student and others in the setting to acclimate to your presence. Collecting data immediately upon arrival in the observation setting is more likely to lead to *reactivity*, a situation in which the target student's behavior is influenced by the measurement procedure itself (Johnston & Pennypacker, 1993). Another common tactic in reducing reactivity is for the observer to position her- or himself in an inconspicuous corner of the room that allows clear access to the observed behavior, but is away from students. It is also recommended that the observer not spend the entire observation period observing the target student but instead vary her or his gaze to other students around the room, so as to not draw undue attention to the target student.

To collect a valid sample of behavior and its environmental predictors and consequences from which to draw conclusions, it is recommended that observations occur on at least two separate occasions and last at least 30 minutes per observation period. Further, at least ten incidents of the behavior should be observed over that period. If fewer than ten incidents are observed in two observation periods, then more observation periods are warranted before summarizing the results of the observation.

Supplementing Systematic Direct Observation with Other Observation

Since the individuals conducting SDOs are not the teachers or staff members who are typically in the natural school environment of the target student, it is a good idea to gather observation data from those in the natural environment. Observation data by teachers or staff members need not be closely structured because these data will simply supplement the more rigorous data collected in structured interviews and SDOs. It is a good practice to provide a form to the teachers or staff that can be used to record behaviors, antecedents, and consequences when they occur. This can be a simple form, like the example in Figure 6.4. When using this form, the teacher or staff member simply writes down what she or he perceives to be the antecedent, behavior, and consequence for each incident of problem behavior and the time and date at which it occurred. There is no need for the teacher or staff member to summarize the data. It will be the behavior team's responsibility to summarize the results and integrate them with the other data gathered in Tier 3. Although this form is relatively simple, it is important to explain its use to teachers and

FBA TEACHER OBSERVATION FORM

STUDENT: _____   OBSERVER: _____

INCIDENT #	DATE & TIME	ANTECEDENT WHAT HAPPENED BEFORE THE BEHAVIOR?	BEHAVIOR WHAT DID THE STUDENT DO?	CONSEQUENCE WHAT DID STUDENT GET OUT OF THE BEHAVIOR?
1				
2				
3				
4				
5				
6				
7				
8				
9				
10				
11				
12				
13				
14				
15				
16				
17				
18				
19				
20				

FIGURE 6.4 Functional Behavioral Assessment Teacher Observation Form.

staff members since many of them will not have much background in behavior theory or the functional model of behavior; thus, they may not naturally understand behavior in the context of antecedents and consequences. Further, it is best practice to visit with the teachers or staff members after a few days to see if they are experiencing any difficulty using the form. Simple FBA observation forms can also be used by caregivers at home. However, the environmental conditions at home are always different from the environmental conditions in a school. Thus, the data from school are generally going to be more useful than data from home when planning interventions in the school context.

Integrating Sources of Data for Precision Hypothesis Statements

By the time that the data collection process in Tier 3 is complete, it is likely that a wealth of information will be available to inform the writing of a precision hypothesis statement. Sources of functional data from Tier 1 include ODRs and archival data. In Tier 2, functional data are collected from simple, unstructured interviews. In Tier 3, functional data include structured interviews with teachers; informal interviews with caregivers; SDOs of antecedents, behaviors, and consequences; and informal ABC observations from teachers and/or staff members. After data collection in Tier 3, the behavior team is tasked with integrating these different data and creating a precision hypothesis statement that can be used to develop an FBA-based BIP.

One of the keys to integrating data from multiple sources is to look for agreements in the data. For example, if FACTS interviews, FBA-OSF observations, and informal interviews all indicate that difficult tasks are the most common antecedent, this is generally sufficient for inclusion in the hypothesis. However, it is likely that some sources of data will lead to differing findings for antecedents, setting events, behaviors, or consequences. In these cases, it is important to focus on the quality of the data. As a general rule of thumb, data collected in later tiers are more accurate than data collected in earlier tiers. If there is consistency in the data from Tier 3 but these data disagree with the informal interviews of Tier 2, the data from Tier 3 should be most relevant for developing the hypothesis.

Perhaps the most complicated situation arises when there is no obvious agreement across data sources. In these cases, it is important to look for underlying themes. Consider a situation in which FACTS interviews indicate that the maintaining consequence is adult attention and the antecedent is independent seatwork, but the FBA-OSF indicates that the maintaining consequence is escape from task and the antecedent is no attention.

Since both situations share the same antecedent (working alone), we can feel confident about our antecedent. The consequence, however, is less clear since escape from task is very different from obtaining adult attention. In this case, it would be reasonable to focus on adult attention as the primary function because it has a logical connection to being alone, with no attention, during independent seatwork. In other words, when no attention has been available for an extended period of time, the value of attention would increase and attention would be more likely to both motivate behavior and function as a reinforcer. Professional judgments of this sort require significant behavioral expertise for the team as they are not intuitively obvious. Ultimately, though, it would be best to look for other sources of data that may confirm one function over the other before writing the precision hypothesis statement. If that proves impossible and a hypothesis is developed based on uncertain data, then it will be important to assess the effectiveness of interventions built off of that hypothesis and make changes to the hypothesis and interventions if they do not lead to an improvement in behavior.

Team-based Process

As with all tiers of FBA, it is essential that the Tier 3 team have behavioral expertise and represent the staff who would be involved with intervention. Behavioral expertise is important for making difficult discriminations between functional and irrelevant antecedents and consequences. For example, before a behavior in an environment, many events occur that could be considered antecedents to the behavior. However, only *some* of those events or stimuli have an effect on the behavior. Making these discriminations can be very difficult for people who have limited or no background in behavior theory or direct observation skills. Further, Bennazi, Horner, and Good (2006) found that teams with at least one person who has behavioral expertise developed more technically adequate interventions based on FBA findings. This study also found that it is important to have a team with representative staff, in order to develop interventions based on FBA findings that have a high contextual fit. Anderson and Scott (2009) also point out that teams dealing with intense behavior problem should have someone, such as a school administrator, who is capable of allocating school resources.

As summarized in Table 6.1, it is recommended that the team meet at least once before FBA data collection begins in Tier 3, once during the data collection process, and once after data are collected. During the first meeting the team should review the precision hypothesis statement developed in Tier 2,

Table 6.1 The team meeting process for tier 3 functional behavioral assessment (FBA)

Meetings	Tasks	Duration

1. Pre–data collection planning	• Review the data and precision hypothesis statement developed from previous tiers
	• Assign data collection responsibilities
	  o Interviews
	  o Observation
	• Schedule next meeting
		≈ 30 minutes

2. Mid–data collection fidelity check	• Review fidelity of data collection • Develop a plan to ensure that all data are collected properly by final meeting • Schedule next meeting	≈ 30 minutes
3. Data summary and behavior intervention plan writing	• Develop a precision hypothesis statement based on all data gathered in Tiers 1, 2, and 3. • Develop an FBA-based behavior intervention plan	≈ 90 minutes

assign data collection responsibilities, and schedule future meetings. By reviewing the previous precision hypothesis statement, the team will have a hypothesis to consider during data collection and a starting point for determining which behaviors are most likely to be reported and observed. When assigning data collection responsibilities, it is likely that only a few team members with behavioral expertise will be directly involved in collecting data. In particular, structured interviews and SDOs should be completed by those with behavioral expertise. If other sources of data are planned, such as student interviews or parent interviews, then these can be opportunities for other members of the team to get involved.

The meeting convened during the data collection process should focus on fidelity of the data collection process. For example, if the social worker has agreed to do the FACTS interview, and the school psychologist has agreed to conduct the SDO, these team members should report their progress and the

TASK	DATE COMPLETED
Step 1. Review FBA data from Tier 1 and Tier 2 and the precision hypothesis statement from Tier 2 for the target student.	

Step 2. Develop a data collection plan for Tier 3 that includes:
        a. semi-structured interviews
        b. systematic direct observation	

Step 3. Collect data from across multiple settings (e.g.,classroom and unstructured setting) and multiple informants (e.g., classroom teacher(s), parents).	
Step 4. Meet as a team to review fidelity of data collection process.	
Step 5. Team reviews data from all tiers and develops a precision hypothesis statement.	
Step 6. Team develops, implements, and monitors an FBA-based behavior intervention plan for the target student (details described in Chapter 7).	

FIGURE 6.5 Tier 3 Functional Behavioral Assessment Fidelity Checklist.

team should decide if any additional support will be necessary to complete data collection in a timely manner so that intervention can begin as soon as possible. If data collection is complete by the time of the second meeting, then the processes of developing a new precision hypothesis statement and developing interventions can begin.

During the third meeting, the team will summarize the results of the FBA into a precision hypothesis statement and begin developing the FBA-based BIP. The team process of developing and implementing interventions in Tier 3 will be reviewed in Chapter 7.

Summary

In Chapter 6, we reviewed the data collection and team decision-making processes for Tier 3 FBAs. Data collected in Tier 3 include semi-structured interviews (with an emphasis on the FACTS) and SDOs (with an emphasis on the FBA-OSF). Team processes include the integration of sources of data from across all three tiers into a precision hypothesis statement and the organization of team meetings to ensure the collection of high-quality data. A fidelity checklist is included here to guide the process of Tier 3 FBAs (Figure 6.5). Chapter 7 will address how to use the data collected from all three tiers to develop and implement an effective FBA-based BIP for an individual student.

7

■■■

Behavior Intervention Plans Based on Tier 3 Functional Behavioral Assessments

The purpose for conducting a functional behavioral assessment (FBA) is to develop an effective intervention. The investment involved in conducting FBAs is only justified when FBAs lead to measurable outcomes for the students involved. Unfortunately, not every assessment process used in schools is designed to lead to effective interventions. For example, when a student is referred for special education, schools are mandated to complete a comprehensive evaluation to determine whether or not the student qualifies for special education services. If the student qualifies for services based on the special education assessment process, then an individualized education plan (IEP) is developed. However, the assessment data that were collected in the evaluation process are not designed to inform the interventions that schools should implement for students who have IEPs (Gresham & Witt, 1997; Reschly & Tilly, 1999). The intervention focus of the FBA process can therefore be contrasted with models of assessment that serve primarily to categorize students, such as the cognitive assessment and behavior rating scales used in special education evaluations.

As noted in Chapter 2, there is evidence that FBAs lead to effective interventions (Ervin et al., 2001). Further, recent studies have found that interventions based on the information gathered in an FBA are more effective than behavioral interventions not based on FBAs (Filter & Horner, 2009; Ingram, Lewis-Palmer, & Sugai, 2005; Newcomer & Lewis, 2004). Therefore, FBAs have been demonstrated to have treatment validity.

Although evidence suggests that FBAs lead to effective interventions, the process of connecting FBA findings to interventions can be difficult, but critical in maximizing the effectiveness of interventions. A number of elements are involved in this process including knowing what interventions are best for specific functions of behavior, selecting the most technically adequate interventions based on the FBA findings with the most contextual fit, writing goals and measuring outcomes, and ensuring that interventions are implemented with fidelity. We will begin by addressing the matching of interventions to functions of behavior.

Appropriate Interventions for Various Functions of Behavior

A comprehensive coverage of specific interventions that have been demonstrated to be effective for various functions of behavior is beyond the scope of this book. Instead, we focus on general strategies with a few specific examples. For more comprehensive reviews of effective behavioral interventions and how they relate to various functions of behavior, please see Cooper, Heron, and Heward (2007) or Chandler and Dahlquist (2010).

The conditions that will be manipulated in an FBA-based behavior intervention plan (BIP) will be the same as the conditions identified in the FBA that predict and maintain problem behavior—setting events, antecedents, behaviors, and consequences. In other words, BIPs should be based on setting event manipulations, antecedent manipulations, behavior manipulations (i.e., teaching behavior), and consequence manipulations. Table 7.1 summarizes these strategies, and each is explained in more detail below.

Setting Event Manipulations

The logic of setting event manipulations is well-illustrated in a study by Kennedy and Itkonen (1993). These researchers described those setting events that were occasioning the problem behavior of two students and the setting event manipulations that successfully reduced the problem behaviors. Although the specific setting events and manipulations reported in the study are not broadly generalizable to any behavior, the method used develop setting event manipulations based on the assessment results is relevant to any situation. Using the FBA methods described in Chapter 6, Kennedy and Itkonen found that, in the first case, a high school girl with severe disabilities had significantly more problem behaviors on days when she awakened more than 5 minutes late in the morning than on days when she didn't. To reduce this setting event, the staff working with this student set up a plan whereby (a) she was responsible for turning off the morning alarm herself, and (b) she could choose her breakfast and clothes if she woke up less than 5 minutes

---

Table 7.1 Summary of functional behavioral assessment (FBA)-based behavior interventions

Setting Event Manipulations	Antecedent Manipulations	Behavior Manipulations (Behavior Teaching Strategies)	Consequence Manipulations
• Eliminate setting events. • Neutralize setting events. • Noncontingent reinforcement (NCR)	• Eliminate antecedents. • Add prompt for appropriate behavior.	• Select and teach a replacement behavior using behavioral skills training.	• Reinforce appropriate behaviors. • Extinguish/ignore inappropriate behaviors. • Punish inappropriate behaviors.*

*Since FBAs do not inform the selection of punishment interventions, and punishment is associated with several risks, punishment is not recommended for FBA-based behavior intervention plans except under limited circumstances.

after the alarm sounded. This intervention was shown to completely eliminate the setting event, and disruptive behavior dropped to extremely low levels. It should be noted that the level of behavior during intervention matched the level of behavior that was observed on mornings when the setting event naturally did not occur. With a second female high school student with severe disabilities, the researchers found that the setting event was the route that an aide took when driving the student to school. In specific, the in-town route was associated with high levels of problem behavior during the school day and the highway route was associated with significantly less problem behavior. The setting event manipulation implemented ensured that the aide always used the highway route in the morning by eliminating errands that required her to drive the in-town route. Once again, the same significant pattern of behavior change was observed. With both students, the relationship between the setting event manipulations and the decrease in problem behavior was demonstrated using sound experimental design.

The Kennedy and Itkonen (1993) study demonstrated the general method of *eliminating setting events*, which is applicable to any setting event. In this strategy, a setting event is identified through the FBA process and then steps are taken to ensure that the setting event does not occur. This strategy can be very effective but is not always practical because some setting events are beyond the control of the school. For example, if a student is found to have more problem behaviors on days after he stays overnight with his father, it may not be possible to prevent him from spending nights at his father's house. In a case such as this, it is reasonable to consider other setting event manipulations, such as neutralizing setting events or noncontingent reinforcement.

Horner, Day, and Day (1997) demonstrated that you can minimize the effects of setting events on behavior by using a strategy called a *neutralizing routine*. The general idea of a neutralizing routine is to implement an intervention after a setting event occurs in an attempt to defuse the situation. For example, if a student comes to school lacking attention at home, we can expect that any behavior that leads to more attention will be more likely to occur at school, even if that involves problem behavior. To neutralize this situation, someone in the school could meet with the student early in the morning and provide a few minutes of attention. Or, if a student is known to be more likely to engage in problem behavior after failing an academic task, then the teacher could neutralize this setting event by giving the student a task on which he will be highly successful immediately after failing an academic task.

Similar to the idea of a neutralizing routine is an intervention called *noncontingent reinforcement* (NCR; Cooper et al., 2007). Despite the fact that NCR includes the word reinforcement, it is in fact a setting event manipulation. NCR involves providing the maintaining reinforcer on a regular basis, regardless of whether problem behavior occurs. For example, if an FBA indicates that a student's problem behavior is maintained by escape from a difficult task, an NCR would involve giving the student a short break from difficult tasks every few minutes. Or, if a student's problem behavior is maintained by teacher attention, then the teacher could engage in brief interactions with the student every few minutes. The logic of this intervention is that it will reduce the value of the reinforcer that has maintained the behavior by offering a lot of it before behavior occurs. A simple analogy is that a person should be considerably less likely to eat an unhealthy dessert if she or he has been completely filled up by a meal. NCR works by removing a condition of deprivation that would otherwise motivate behavior. NCR is such a simple intervention that we recommend its use whenever possible. It is a prevention strategy that can be very efficient and effective.

Antecedent Manipulations

Antecedent manipulations generally fit into two categories: eliminating antecedents for problem behavior, and adding prompts for appropriate behavior. When *eliminating antecedents for problem behavior*, it is important to identify what antecedents in the environment are triggering problem behavior by completing an FBA. Once the antecedent(s) has been identified, a plan is developed to eliminate the antecedent(s). Without the antecedent, the problem behavior becomes irrelevant (Crone & Horner, 2003). For example, if a student's problem behavior is preceded by commands from a nonfavored adult, then we can assume that there would be no reason for the behavior to occur if no nonfavored adults are issuing commands. Several researchers have reviewed the most common antecedents to problem behaviors in classrooms, such as task difficulty, mode of instruction, student interest in materials, pace of instruction, choice, and wanted or unwanted attention (Filter, 2004; Kern & Clemens, 2007; Munk & Repp, 1994). In each of these cases, it is possible to eliminate the problematic component of the antecedent. For example, if the antecedent for a student's problem behavior is difficult academic tasks, then the student's skills could be matched more appropriately with the curriculum, so that it is no longer too difficult. Or, if the antecedent for a student's problem behavior is unwanted attention from the teacher, then directions could be given by an instructional aide rather than by the teacher.

Another antecedent manipulation is *adding prompts for appropriate behavior*. By reminding students which behaviors are expected and will lead to the best consequences, it is expected that those behavior will be more likely to occur than the problem behavior. For example, if we remind a student to raise her or his hand rather than shout in class, then we would expect that shouting would be less likely to occur and hand-raising would be more likely to occur. However, this strategy requires that an appropriate alternative to the problem behavior has been identified and taught, and that the appropriate behavior leads to a desired consequence, preferably the same reinforcer as that which has maintained problem behavior. Establishing alternative replacement behaviors and setting up reinforcement systems for them will be discussed under the sections *behavior manipulations (behavior teaching strategies)* and *consequence strategies* below.

Behavior Manipulations (Behavior Teaching Strategies)

The problem behavior identified during an FBA occurs because it is prompted by an antecedent and maintained by a reinforcer. One way to eliminate this relationship is to identify a *replacement behavior* that can be prompted by the same antecedent and maintained by the same reinforcer as the problem behavior, thereby providing an alternative route for accessing the reinforcer. Replacement behaviors need to not only serve the same function as the problem behavior but should also require less effort than the problem behavior (Sugai, Lewis-Palmer, & Hagen, 1998). By requiring less effort, it is more likely that the student with the problem behavior will choose to engage in the replacement behavior than in the more effortful problem behavior to obtain the same consequence.

After a replacement behavior has been selected, it is important to ensure that the behavior has been taught. If the student already engages in the replacement behavior some of the time, then she or he should only need to be reminded to use it with a prompt, as described in the previous section. If the student has not engaged in the behavior in the past, then she or he needs to be directly taught the behavior via a simple process of behavioral skills teaching. Behavioral skills teaching involves the following steps: (a) describe the replacement behavior, (b) demonstrate the replacement behavior, (c) have the student directly practice the replacement behavior, and (d) provide feedback on whether the replacement behavior occurred as expected (Miltenberger, 2004). After the replacement behavior has been demonstrated to occur correctly, it is then important to remind the student to engage in that replacement behavior whenever the antecedent for problem behavior occurs.

To clarify the process of selecting and teaching replacement behaviors, we will provide two examples. Consider a case in which an FBA has indicated that the problem behavior is using inappropriate language in class, the antecedent to the behavior is independent seatwork, and the consequence (reinforcer) is obtaining adult attention. An appropriate replacement behavior could be raising a hand because it would require less effort than yelling, is more socially appropriate, and could be used to obtain the teacher's attention. The student would be taught to raise her hand when she wants attention during independent seatwork. Another example is a case in which the problem behavior is pushing/hitting peers, the antecedent is being approached by a nonfavored peer, and the consequence (reinforcer) is escaping peer attention. An appropriate replacement behavior could be telling the nonfavored peer to leave her or him alone because telling a peer to leave her or him alone would require less effort than pushing/hitting a peer, is more socially appropriate, and should lead to escape from the peer's attention (i.e., the peer would leave her or him alone). In this case, the student would be taught to use words whenever a nonfavored peer approaches her or him and she or he wants to be left alone.

Consequence Manipulations

There are three basic ways to manipulate consequences based on FBAs: (a) reinforce appropriate behaviors, (b) extinguish/ignore inappropriate behaviors, and (c) punish inappropriate behaviors. These manipulations have been intentionally listed in order of their recommended use. In other words, in keeping with a preventative and positive perspective of behavior management, we strongly recommend using reinforcement of appropriate behaviors before or instead of punishment and the use of extinction/ignoring as preferable to punishment as a strategy to decrease problem behavior.

The strategy of *reinforcing appropriate behaviors* is closely tied to the replacement behavior described in the previous section in that it involves providing the maintaining consequence identified in an FBA as the reinforcer each time the replacement behavior occurs. This specific technique has been described in the literature as differential reinforcement of alternative behaviors (DRA; Cooper et al., 2007). In other words, if the FBA identified that problem behavior is maintained by obtaining adult attention, then adult attention would be provided whenever the replacement behavior occurs. As long as adult attention is delivered more often when the replacement behavior occurs than when the problem behavior occurs, the replacement behavior will become more frequent than the problem behavior. So, regularly reinforcing the replacement behavior will reduce the problem behavior.

Reinforcement of appropriate behaviors does not require that the reinforcer used be the same reinforcer that was identified in the FBA as maintaining the problem behavior. The advantage of using the reinforcer from the FBA is that we know that that reinforcer is effective in maintaining the student's behavior, assuming that the appropriate setting events have occurred. When other reinforcers are selected, we are less certain of their value to the individual. One common strategy for reinforcing appropriate behaviors is the *token economy*, wherein students receive small reinforcers (tokens) that can be exchanged for larger reinforcers, such as privileges or tangibles (e.g., pencils, small toys). In general, token economies are effective for most students, but it is important to determine what larger reinforcers will be of interest to the student.

Extinguishing/ignoring problem behaviors involves a planned effort to withhold reinforcement when the problem behavior occurs. For example, if an FBA indicates that a problem behavior is maintained by peer attention, then extinction would involve ensuring that peers do not react when a problem behavior occurs. One simple and elegant intervention that can be used for these situations is called the "concentration game" (Sprague & Golly, 2005). The concentration game involves challenging all of the students in a class to see who can go the longest without laughing or reacting to the misbehavior of others and providing group rewards if they do well. Another example of extinction/ignoring is a case in which a student whose behavior is maintained by escape from a difficult task is required to complete the task regardless of her or his behavior (i.e., not allowed to get out of the task). This could involve completing the task after school or during recess if not during the regular task time.

Punishing problem behavior involves providing an unfavorable consequence whenever a problem behavior occurs. Punishment is attempted quite frequently in schools when students are sent to the office and/or suspended from school when problem behaviors occur. Unfortunately, this strategy is overused and is sometimes ineffective because consequences that seem like punishments may not in fact be punishments at all. For example, students whose problem behaviors are maintained by escape from tasks are far more likely to increase problem behaviors when they result in being sent to the office during instructional time than they are to decrease problem behavior. This is because getting out of the instructional tasks is what they wanted in the first place (i.e., it is the escape reinforcer for the problem behavior). Therefore, attempted punishment is not always actual punishment. Other risks in the use of punishment to decrease behavior include the fact that suppression of one behavior can lead to increase in other problem behaviors, students avoiding the person who delivers punishment, and emotional outbursts (Cooper et al., 2007). Finally, it should be noted that an FBA does not tell us what punishments are likely to be effective—it only tells us which consequences are *unlikely* to work as punishers. Since the FBA process does not inform the use of punishment, and punishment is associated with several risks that are often not worth taking, we encourage the use of reinforcement of appropriate behaviors and extinction/ignoring over punishment and do not provide specific suggestions for using punishment. For guidelines on the ethical use of punishment procedures, readers are directed to Miltenberger (2004).

Functional Behavioral Assessment

Selecting Appropriate Interventions for an FBA-based Behavior Intervention Plan

Now that we have covered some interventions that are relevant to various functions of behavior, the next step in developing a solid FBA-based BIP (FBA-BIP) is selecting the most technically adequate and contextually appropriate interventions to include in the plan. An FBA-BIP should include at least one setting event manipulation, one antecedent manipulation, one behavior manipulation (behavior teaching strategy), and one consequence strategy. Given that there is more than one possible intervention for each of these categories, the FBA team will be responsible for developing a few possible interventions for each category and then selecting from among those possible interventions. We begin with the process of developing possible interventions and then cover the process of selecting from among them for the FBA-BIP.

Developing Possible Interventions

After all three tiers of FBA data collection have been completed, the team should have summarized the findings into a clear precision hypothesis statement that describes the setting events, antecedents, behaviors, and consequences. For the purposes of developing interventions, it is practical to write out the setting events, antecedents, behaviors, and consequences into separate boxes, as shown in the form *Developing Interventions for FBA-BIPs* (Figure 7.1). Under these FBA summary boxes, room is available in the form for listing several specific interventions that could address each of these four terms. When working with this form, it is suggested that interventions be described precisely (e.g., teacher provides brief attention to the student every 5 minutes regardless of behavior) rather than using their corresponding broad terms that were described in the previous section (e.g., NCR). However, many of the logistics of implementation (e.g., how the teacher is trained, the settings in which the intervention will occur) do not need to be addressed in this stage of the process as these will be addressed after specific interventions are chosen for inclusion in the FBA-BIP. The interventions to be included in the Developing Interventions for FBA-BIPs form can be developed in a brainstorming session with the team. During this brainstorming session, it is more important to develop many interventions than it is to develop the best interventions.

Selecting From Among Possible Interventions

After the Developing Interventions form (Figure 7.1) has been completed, then the team will decide which interventions are most appropriate for actual

	SETTING EVENT(S)	ANTECEDENT(S)	BEHAVIOR(S)	CONSEQUENCE(S)
FBA SUMMARY	⇨	⇨	⇨	
POSSIBLE INTERVENTIONS	SETTING EVENT MANIPULATIONS • _____ • _____ • _____ • _____	ANTECEDENT MANIPULATIONS • _____ • _____ • _____ • _____	BEHAVIOR MANIPULATIONS • _____ • _____ • _____ • _____	CONSEQUENCE MANIPULATIONS • _____ • _____ • _____ • _____

Directions: Fill in the setting events, antecedents, behaviors, and consequence based on the results from the FBA. Then for each of the four terms from the FBA (setting events, antecedents, behaviors, and consequences), the team should list at least 3 possible interventions that should reasonably be expected to improve behavior. The team will then select at least one intervention/ manipulation for each of the four terms for inclusion in the FBA-BIP.

FIGURE 7.1 Developing interventions for functional behavior assessment–based behavior intervention plans (FBA-BIPs).

inclusion in the FBA-BIP by taking into account technical adequacy and contextual fit. As was the case with the process of combining sources of data from an FBA into one precision hypothesis statement, the process of selecting from among possible interventions developed for an FBA-BIP can be complicated and requires professional judgment on the part of the team.

The issue of technical adequacy is addressed by asking whether there is reason to believe that any of the interventions generated on the Developing Interventions form are more likely to be successful than others based on scientific evidence. For example, NCR has a large literature base validating its use (Tucker, Sigafoos, & Bushell, 1998; Vollmer & Borrero, 2009), whereas an intervention such as prompting appropriate behavior has a much smaller literature base. Therefore, the team could conclude that NCR is more likely to be effective than is prompting appropriate behavior, even though both are reasonable interventions, given the results of an FBA.

The issue of contextual fit can be complex but relates primarily to issues of local values, resources, and skills (Albin, Luchysyn, Horner, & Flannery, 1996). In regards to values, the team may know that the people likely to implement the FBA-BIP are opposed to the use of reinforcements to improve behavior, in which case the use of a token system for reinforcing behavior may not be likely to be implemented with fidelity and would therefore be better left off of the FBA-BIP. Resources may include time or money, so that a focus on resources would favor interventions that require the least amount of effort or financial investment to obtain the best outcomes. Finally, the existing skills of the interventionists (i.e., the teachers or staff who will be delivering the FBA-BIP) will affect selection, such that interventions that require significant behavior management skills on the part of the interventionist may not be as feasible as those that do not require these skills. So, the issues of technical adequacy and contextual fit are both important for the development of a quality FBA-BIP. Benazzi, Horner, and Good (2006) found that technical adequacy and contextual fit were best addressed by teams that included behavioral expertise to ensure technical adequacy, and representative membership (e.g., teachers, administrators, staff) to ensure contextual fit.

After this selection process, the FBA-BIP should include at least one setting event manipulation, one antecedent manipulation, one behavior manipulation (behavior teaching strategy), and one consequence manipulation. Although one consequence manipulation is considered a minimal criterion, we recommend that the two consequence manipulations of differential reinforcement of appropriate replacement behavior and extinction/ignoring of problem behavior be included in the FBA-BIP. This will ensure that the replacement behavior is more effective than the problem behavior, because the replacement behavior will be reinforced but the problem behavior will not. As noted earlier in the chapter, we also recommend that NCR be included in most FBA-BIPs because it is a simple, highly effective intervention. Ultimately, it is best to keep the FBA-BIP to no more than five or six specific interventions because attempts to implement more than six interventions for a particular student are likely to lead to difficulties with fidelity of implementation. In other words, too many interventions may be too complicated to implement well.

After specific interventions have been selected and described in the FBA-BIP, it is necessary to assign someone to be in charge of the implementation of each intervention. Assigning implementers to specific interventions should decrease the likelihood that any of the interventions will not be implemented due to diffusion of responsibility. Further, each person assigned as an implementer should be supported by the team, so that the intervention details are clear to her or him and training and support are available to her or him if the intervention is something with which the implementer has no experience.

FBA-BASED BEHAVIOR INTERVENTION PLAN (FBA-BIP)

STUDENT NAME _____

TEAM MEMBERS _____

SUMMARY OF FBA

FBA COMPLETION DATE _____

DATA COLLECTORS _____

SOURCES OF DATA

RECORD REVIEW ☐   TEACHER INTERVIEW(S) ☐   GUARDIAN INTERVIEW(S) ☐

STUDENT INTEREVIEW ☐ DIRECT OBSERVATION   ☐   OTHER ☐ _____

	SETTING EVENT(S)	ANTECEDENT(S)	BEHAVIOR(S)	CONSEQUENCE(S)
FBA SUMMARY				

FIGURE 7.2 Functional behavioral assessment–based behavior intervention plan (FBA-BIP).

Figure 7.2 is a format for writing FBA-BIPs that includes a summary of the FBA results (page 1), a place to list and describe interventions as well as assign implementers (page 2), a process for measuring fidelity of implementation and outcomes (page 3), a graph template for monitoring behavior outcomes (page 4), and an action plan for making changes to the plan based on data (page 5). The process for measuring fidelity and outcomes on page 3 will be described in the next section, the process for graphing outcomes on page 4 of the FBA-BIP was described in Chapter 4, and the use of the action plan on page 5 is reviewed in the next section. A completed example of an FBA-BIP is presented near the end of this chapter in Figure 7.3.

BEHAVIOR INTERVENTION PLAN

	INTERVENTION	DETAILED DESCRIPTION OF INTERVENTION	IMPLEMENTER(S)
SETTING EVENT MANIPULATION			
ANTECEDENT MANIPULATION			
BEHAVIOR MANIPULATION			
CONSEQUENCE MANIPULATION			
OTHER (DESCRIBE)			
OTHER (DESCRIBE)			

FIGURE 7.2 Continued.

EVALUATION PLAN

<u>FIDELITY OF IMPLEMENTATION</u>

    PERSON RESPONSIBLE FOR EVALUATION   ————————————————

    DATA TO BE COLLECTED:

	FIDELITY EVALUATION RESULTS			
	DATE:	DATE:	DATE:	DATE:
FIDELITY LEVEL (high, medium, low)				
ACTION TO BE TAKEN				

<u>MEASURABLE OUTCOMES</u>

    PERSON RESPONSIBLE FOR EVALUATION   ————————————————

    DATA TO BE COLLECTED:

SHORT TERM GOAL:

LONG TERM GOAL:

FIGURE 7.2 Continued.

Evaluation Plans for Fidelity of Implementation and Outcomes

The specification, collection, and use of fidelity and outcomes data ensure that the entire process of conducting FBAs and writing an intervention plan leads to positive outcomes for the student involved. A plan that is *not* monitored for implementation and outcomes is one that is of uncertain utility. This situation is all too familiar in many schools, in which intervention plans are written and shared once with the relevant people and are assumed to be happening and working. School teams cannot risk such assumptions. Instead, teams need to monitor fidelity and outcomes, then make intentional decisions to change direction if the data suggest that behavior is not improving (see Table 4.1 in Chapter 4).

          Functional Behavioral Assessment

LINE GRAPH OF BEHAVIOR OUTCOMES

BEHAVIOR MEASURED: _____

MEASUREMENT SYSTEM: _____
(e.g., DBR, SDO)

BEHAVIOR
LEVEL
(Fill in)

	Date:	Date:	Date:	Date:	Date:	Date:	Date:	Date:	Date:	Date:
BASELINE OR INTERVENTION	BL INT	BL INT	BL INT	BL INT	BL INT	BL INT	BL INT	BL INT	BL INT	BL INT

FIGURE 7.2 Continued.

Fidelity of Implementation

To ensure that all elements of a plan are being implemented in the way that they were written in the plan, page 3 of the FBA-BIP (Figure 7.2) includes a section to describe what fidelity data will be collected, who will collect it, and the results of fidelity checks. It is important to specify a particular person who will be responsible for evaluating fidelity, so that it isn't assumed that the team will somehow coordinate its efforts to accomplish this. The data that can be collected to measure fidelity of implementation should be specified, then used for monitoring and decision making on the four separate dates listed on page 3. An efficient way to measure fidelity is to create a checklist of the critical features of each intervention, then either observe if these features

ACTION PLAN FOR FBA-BIP

ACTION	DATE WRITTEN	MEASURABLE GOAL	DATE OF REVIEW	GOAL MET? (CIRCLE)	
				YES	NO
				YES	NO
				YES	NO
				YES	NO
				YES	NO
				YES	NO
				YES	NO

FIGURE 7.2 Continued.

are in place or interview the person responsible for implementing each piece using the checklist. Direct observation is going to be a more valid measurement approach, but interviews are more efficient.

The levels of fidelity of implementation on the FBA-BIP form (Figure 7.2) are simplified to a rating of high, medium, or low. Although this approach to rating fidelity is not precise, it is applicable to any method of measuring fidelity. We recommend considering high fidelity to mean more than 90% of features are being implemented properly, medium fidelity to mean 50% to 89% of features are being implemented properly, and low fidelity to mean less than 50% of features are being implemented properly. When fidelity of implementation is high, then no actions need to be taken to improve fidelity. When fidelity is medium or low, then the team should take action to

Functional Behavioral Assessment

improve fidelity. This will generally involve ongoing consultation with the implementers to support their efforts. In some cases, use of the behavioral skills teaching approach described in this chapter may be necessary when working with adult implementers if they lack the skills for proper implementation. If the low level of implementation is more an apparent result of lack of motivation on the part of the implementer, then the person assigned to monitor fidelity should develop a strategy to increase implementer motivation (e.g., remind them of the benefits in terms of reduced behavior problems or offer praise whenever quality implementation is observed). It is recommended that the plan be implemented as written until the outcomes data indicate that a high-fidelity intervention plan is not working.

Outcomes: Writing Goals and Measuring Progress

To determine if the efforts invested in the FBA and FBA-BIP process lead to improvements in student behavior, it is necessary to define a system for measuring behavior, specify goals using the measurement system, and monitor outcomes using a graphed format. Pages 3 and 4 of the FBA-BIP (Figure 7.2) include places to develop a measurement system, write goals, and graph progress.

The data to be collected for monitoring behavior outcomes generally fall into the two general categories, as described in Chapter 4: systematic direct observation (SDO) and direct behavior ratings (DBRs). The specific behavior to be measured should be described in the plan. The behavior and its operational definition should be derived from the previous FBA process for the student. If, for example, the problem behavior assessed in the FBA was fighting, then an operational definition for fighting should have been created during the FBA, and fighting is the behavior that should be measured in the FBA-BIP.

The FBA-BIP should specify short- and long-term goals. The process of writing short- and long-term goals was covered in detail in Chapter 4.

Action Planning

Data should be accompanied by a decision-making process. Therefore, when the fidelity or outcomes data collected suggest that the team needs to do something differently, then this needs to be documented on an action plan like the one on page 5 of the FBA-BIP (Figure 7.2). When developing action plan items, the team should clearly specify what action is to be taken, the goal for the action, a review date, and whether the action led to the desired goal. The advantage to using an action plan attached to the actual FBA-BIP is that decisions are documented and the team is then accountable to those decisions. Without action plan, data-based decisions may be made but will be unlikely to be implemented or monitored.

Home–School Collaboration

Family involvement has been described in the FBA data collection process through interviews and permissions, and the next step of family member involvement is to include them in the intervention. It is important to make this home–school connection from both a values-based and a practical perspective. The values-based perspective is the assumption that it is in the best interest of all involved to have the school supporting the family and the family supporting the school. This value is inherent in school social work. From a practical perspective, the findings of the FBA can be used to help improve behavior problems at home. For example, if the FBA indicates that the student's problem behavior is maintained by obtaining adult attention, then the team could describe how to implement a preventative NCR procedure at home by attending to the student on a regular basis and/or use the consequence-based DRA procedure of providing attention contingent on the replacement behavior that has been taught at school. This is a good role for a school social worker as they have particular training in communicating school processes to parents.

The potential benefits to including family are apparent, but it should be noted that behavior is context-specific, which means that the relationship between behaviors and the environment may be different at home than they are in the school. Therefore, a well-designed school-based FBA-BIP is of indeterminate value in predicting behavior improvements at home even when elements are implemented by the family. The best way to develop an intervention at home is to conduct an FBA that involves systematic direct observations in the home and more in-depth interviews with parents. The forms and procedural details in this book have been intentionally developed with a focus on the school context, but a well-trained behavior specialist can adapt the procedures to the home context.

Case Example

Figure 7.3 shows a case example of a completed FBA-BIP form for a student named Mario. Note that the team is comprised of several different professionals from the school. Annie S. is a school nurse, Dan H. is a special education teacher, Jason W. is a school psychologist, Olivia M. is Mario's regular teacher, and Rachel Y. is the school social worker.

The FBA from page 1 was completed by the school social worker and the special education teacher. Based on record reviews, teacher interviews, guardian interview, and direct observation, they were able to determine a clear description of the setting events, antecedent, behaviors, and reinforcing consequence.

After brainstorming several setting event manipulations, antecedent manipulations, behavior manipulations, and consequence manipulations, they settled on one intervention for each category, except setting events, for which they included two interventions in the final FBA-BIP (see page 2 of Figure 7.3). Olivia M., the regular classroom teacher, was assigned to implement all of the interventions that were to occur in the classroom: NCR, prompting appropriate behavior, and differential reinforcement of appropriate behavior. Rachel Y., the school social worker, was assigned to implement the behavior teaching strategy of teaching Mario to request assistance or attention using a signal on his desk. She then needed to develop a plan for teaching this skill and worked with Mario one-on-one until he demonstrated that he could use the signal at the appropriate times. Finally, Annie, the school nurse, was assigned the setting event manipulation of administering attention deficit-hyperactivity disorder (ADHD) medications at the school because Mario's problem behavior was often related to having forgotten to take his medications at home. Note that each intervention in the plan is written with enough detail so that the implementers should know exactly what to do.

Rachel Y., the school social worker, met with Mario's parents after the FBA-BIP was developed, to obtain their permission to implement it and to discuss how the results could be used at home. In particular, she received their permission to have the school nurse administer Mario's ADHD medication at school and worked out the plan for getting the medications to the nurse. After discussing the other components of the FBA-BIP, Rachel informed the family that there was strong reason to believe that the interventions would be effective in school but that home-based implementation may or may not be as effective. The family decided that they would attempt to address the attention-function of the behavior by talking to Mario for 10 minutes immediately before school and after school, and they agreed to provide him with as much attention as they reasonably could throughout the day, despite having four other children in their care.

On page 2 of the example FBA-BIP, the team decided to assign the monitoring of fidelity of implementation to Jason W., the school psychologist. Jason is responsible for developing a checklist of the features of each intervention in the FBA-BIP and using that to monitor fidelity. Although not specified on the document, Jason W. created the checklists and then briefly interviewed each implementer to determine which features they were implementing. On October 12, 2011, Jason W. reported that the overall level of fidelity was medium and that the NCR intervention was not being implemented well. To improve this finding, Rachel Y., the social worker, agreed to meet with Olivia to review the procedures. This new plan was documented in the action plan on page 5 of the example form, with the goal that the NCR be implemented with 100% fidelity by the next fidelity check. The next fidelity check by Jason W. on November 17, 2011 indicated that this goal was met, and so that team circled the "yes" box for that action item on the action plan.

Also on page 3 of the example FBA-BIP form, the team specified that Rachel Y., the school social worker, would be responsible for collecting the behavior outcome data. The team decided to monitor shouting and inappropriate language (the behaviors listed on the FBA summary on page 1 of the example) using daily DBRs and weekly SDOs. Since only one graph was used on the form, they decided to only graph the SDO data, and the DBR data were informally reviewed by the team at each meeting. Rachel was responsible for weekly SDOs using the Direct Observation Progress Monitoring System (DOPMS) (see Figure 4.1, Chapter 4). The team decided to use the same measurement system for the short- and long-term goals. Graphed data indicate that Rachel Y. collected three observation data points in the baseline condition before the FBA-BIP was implemented and has so far collected five data points since intervention began. The occurrence of problem behavior has dropped from an average of more than

50% of intervals during baseline to less than 20% of intervals during intervention. Since this meets the short-term goal of a 50% reduction in shouting and inappropriate language by October 31, 2011, no action plan items have been added to improve behavior.

In summary, the team developed a BIP based on the results of an FBA that led to a clear decrease in problem behavior. Only one modification was made along the way, based on some problems with the fidelity of one intervention, and Mario appears to be on his way to meeting his long-term goal.

FBA-BASED BEHAVIOR INTERVENTION PLAN (FBA-BIP)
COMPLETED EXAMPLE

STUDENT NAME   **Mario**

TEAM MEMBERS   **Annie S., Dan H., Jason W., Olivia M. and Rachel Y.**

SUMMARY OF FBA

FBA COMPLETION DATE   **9/15/2011**

DATA COLLECTORS   **Rachel Y. and Jason W.**

SOURCES OF DATA

RECORD REVIEW ☒   TEACHER INTERVIEW(S) ☒   GUARDIAN INTERVIEW(S) ☒
STUDENT INTEREVIEW ☐ DIRECT OBSERVATION   ☒   OTHER ☐ _____

	SETTING EVENT(S)	ANTECEDENT(S)	BEHAVIOR(S)	CONSEQUENCE(S)
FBA SUMMARY	-Lack of attention -Not taking ADHD meds	Independent Seatwork	-Shouting -Inappropriate language	Obtain teacher attention

FIGURE 7.3 Completed example of a functional behavior assessment–based behavior intervention plans (FBA-BIP).

	INTERVENTION	DETAILED DESCRIPTION OF INTERVENTION	IMPLEMENTER(S)
SETTING EVENT MANIPULATION	Non-contigent Reinforcement	Teacher will provide Mario attention every 5 minutes in classroom when a vibrator reminds her. The attention should last about 10 seconds and should be phrased in a positive or neutral form and never in the form of reprimands.	Olivia M.
ANTECEDENT MANIPULATION	Prompt appropriate behavior	Before teacher assigned independent seatwork begins, the teacher will remind Mario that if he needs assistance or needs to talk to the teacher, then he should use his desk signal (see behavior manipulation below).	Olivia M.
BEHAVIOR MANIPULATION	Request assistance or attention	When Mario needs assistance or attention during independent seatwork, he will lift a sign on his desk and the teacher will respond. This sign will be created and the procedure will be taught by the school social worker.	Rachel Y.
CONSEQUENCE MANIPULATION	Differential reinforcement of appropriate behavior	When Mario uses his signal during independent seatwork, the teacher will provide attention within 1 minute. Attention will last no more than 30 seconds.	Olivia M.
OTHER (DESCRIBE) Setting Event	ADHD medications administerred at school	Mario will stop into the nurse's office each morning to receive his ADHD medication. Nurse will contact parent if Mario does not come in by 8:15am.	Annie S.

EVALUATION PLAN

FIDELITY OF IMPLEMENTATION

PERSON RESPONSIBLE FOR EVALUATION ___Jason W.___

DATA TO BE COLLECTED: A checklist of critical features for each intervention in the FBA-BIP will be developed and the school psychologist will check with each implementer to determine if features are being implemented consistently.

	FIDELITY EVALUATION RESULTS			
	DATE: 10-12-11	DATE: 11-7-11	DATE:	DATE:
FIDELITY LEVEL (high, medium, low)	Medium	High		
ACTION TO BE TAKEN	Rachel will review NCR procedure with Olivia			

FIGURE 7.3 Continued.

MEASURABLE OUTCOMES

PERSON RESPONSIBLE FOR EVALUATION   __Rachel Y.__

DATA TO BE COLLECTED: **Daily teacher direct behavior ratings (DBRs) for shouting and inappropriate language and weekly SDOs of the same behavior using the DOPMS data will be graphed.**

SHORT TERM GOAL: **50% reduction in shouting and inappropriate language from baseline by 10-31-2011.**

LONG TERM GOAL: **80% reduction in shouting and inappropriate language from baseline by 2-1-2012.**

LINE GRAPH OF BEHAVIOR OUTCOMES

BEHAVIOR MEASURED: **Shouting and inappropriate language**

MEASUREMENT SYSTEM: **Momentary time sampling with DOPMS**
(e.g., DBR, SDO)

BEHAVIOR
LEVEL
(Fill in)

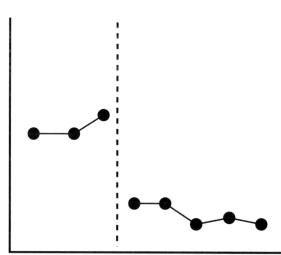

	Date: 9–19	Date: 9–26	Date: 10–3	Date: 10–10	Date: 10–17	Date: 10–24	Date: 10–31	Date: 11–7	Date:	Date:
BASELINE OR INTERVENTION	BL INT	BL INT	BL INT	BL (INT)	BL (INT)	BL (INT)	BL (INT)	BL (INT)	BL INT	BL INT

FIGURE 7.3 Continued.

ACTION PLAN FOR FBA-BIP

ACTION	DATE WRITTEN	MEASURABLE GOAL	DATE OF REVIEW	GOAL MET? (CIRCLE)	
Rachel will review NCR plan with Olivia	**10-12-11**	**NCR will be implemented with 100% fidelity by next fidelity check**	**11-7-11**	(YES)	NO
				YES	NO
				YES	NO
				YES	NO
				YES	NO
				YES	NO
				YES	NO

FIGURE 7.3 Continued.

Summary

The purpose of conducting FBAs is to develop effective interventions and this chapter was focused on developing and implementing individual FBA-BIPs for Tier 3. Processes reviewed include matching interventions to the results of a Tier 3 FBA, selecting interventions for inclusion in an FBA-BIP, and writing FBA-BIPs that include plans for measuring and ensuring fidelity of implementation and behavior outcomes. Figure 7.4 is a fidelity checklist that teams can use when developing Tier 3 FBA-BIPs.

TASK	DATE COMPLETED
Step 1. Review precision hypothesis statement from Tier 3.	
Step 2. As a team, brainstorm interventions using the form, *Developing Interventions for FBA-BIPs* (Figure 7.1)	

Step 3. Select interventions from among those developed in the brainstorming session for inclusion in the FBA-BIP.
a. Consider technical adequacy and contextual fit
b. Select at least one of each of the following:
   i.   Setting event manipulation
   ii. Antecedent manipulation
   iii. Behavior manipulation
   iv. Consequence manipulation
c. Assign implementers for each intervention	

Step 4. Develop evaluation plan that addresses behavior outcomes and fidelity of implementation a. Specify which data will be collected, when it will be collected, and by whom it will be collected.	
Step 5. Establish short-term and long-term behavior goals.	
Step 6. Monitor behavior outcomes and fidelity of implementation and develop action plans for any areas that are in need of improvement. a. Record outcomes date on a line graph	
Step 7. Ensure that everything in the *FBA-BIP* form (Figure 7.2) has been completed that the action plan document is being used when decisions are made about the plan.	

FIGURE 7.4 Tier 3 functional behavior assessment–based behavior intervention plans (FBA-BIP) fidelity checklist.

8

∎∎∎∎

Three-Tiered Functional Behavioral Assessment: Summary and Example

Functional behavioral assessment (FBA) is a team-based process that can improve the behavior of all students in a school when applied in a three-tiered prevention model and used as the basis for developing interventions that are monitored for fidelity and effectiveness. Although the specific populations targeted and specific assessment procedures employed differ across tiers, FBA always involves identifying the environmental conditions that predict and maintain problem behavior, and it always leads to the development of a precision hypothesis statement that informs the development of an effective intervention.

As FBA is applied to ever more intense problems and tiers of support, the process shifts from support planning for all students in a school to the intensive assessment of individual students. In Tier 1, existing behavior data, such as office discipline referrals (ODRs), are analyzed for patterns of antecedents, behaviors, and consequences that occur in the general student population. In Tier 2, students at risk are targeted, and the data collected include brief interviews in addition to comprehensive reviews of existing data. In Tier 3, semi-structured interviews and direct observations are conducted to plan supports for students with significant behavior problems. By allocating more resources to each successive tier as warranted by behavioral need, supports can be offered to more students than are typically served in a school, and overall levels of problem behaviors in schools can be decreased (Walker et al., 1996). FBA was developed for use with individuals with disabilities and significant behavior problems (Hanley, Iwata, & McCord, 2003) but has now evolved to work within the broad structure of schools.

Throughout this book, a number of themes were highlighted and we shall briefly revisit and expand on each of them.

- *A contextual/environmental perspective on student behavior*: Behavior is understood to be the result of an interaction between an individual and the environment. FBA is the process of understanding which conditions in the environment are currently controlling the problem behavior(s) of interest. This focus of all FBA procedures (e.g., interviews, observations, records reviews) is to identify antecedents and consequences to problem behavior, in order to change the antecedents and consequences and thereby change the behavior.

- *FBAs as relevant to all students*: FBA has traditionally been used only with students who have severe problem behavior. The technology has now been adapted over time to help support the behavior of

  all students, including those without disabilities and with minor problem behavior. The adaptations have been to the intensity and efficiency of the assessments but not to the primary focus of assessing antecedents and consequences of problem behavior.

- *FBA as a general education process with relevance to special education*: Many school-based professionals, such as school social workers, are primarily familiar with FBA as it relates to federal special education law (reviewed in Chapter 2). However, FBA is not a process for identifying disabilities but is a procedure that identifies the causes of problem behavior and informs interventions designed to improve student behavior. Since students without disabilities also demonstrate problem behavior, FBA is relevant to improving the behavior of students who are not being considered for or served by special education services.

- *Chapters organized around the three tiers of a prevention model*: The three-tiered model of prevention was reviewed in Chapter 2, and all chapters describing FBA procedures were labeled according to the tiers. This was done to clarify the FBA process on procedural grounds, such as when it is most efficient to gather indirect interview information as opposed to direct observation data. However, the underlying concepts of FBA are stable across tiers, and it is important to note that alternative procedures could be used to accomplish the goals of FBA regardless of tier.

- *The preservation of assessment information across all tiers of prevention*: To make FBAs efficient, it is important to consider all existing data relevant to setting events, antecedents, and consequences of problem behavior, rather than beginning fresh at each tier. When conducting a Tier 2 FBA, ODR data and intervention response data from Tier 1 should be considered. When conducting a Tier 3 FBA, interview data, record review data, and intervention response data from Tier 2 should be considered in addition to the ODR data and intervention response data from Tier 1. By the time an individualized FBA-based behavior intervention plan (FBA-BIP) has been developed and implemented in Tier 3, teams should have significant amounts of data from multiple sources for the target student.

- *FBA as a team-managed process*: Although school social workers make significant contributions to the FBA process, they should be members of a broad team responsible for the process. The same team may be responsible for managing FBAs across all three tiers, or a school may have separate teams for each tier. As a general rule of thumb, it is important to have the same team managing Tier 2 and Tier 3 since both involve individual student behavior planning (Anderson & Scott, 2009). The team should be comprised of at least one person with behavior expertise, another person with control over school resources, and one or more people familiar with the school context. The team should meet regularly, divide responsibilities between meetings, and share responsibility for decision making at meetings. The involvement of the whole team should improve fidelity of the process and ensure that the process continues even if one or two members of a team are reassigned.

Three-tiered Case Example

To summarize the main ideas from the book and to demonstrate the team-based FBA process across all tiers, we offer a case example of a student named Samuel. Although case examples were imbedded in some chapters throughout the book (middle and high school), this elementary case example will take the reader through the entire process across all three tiers.

Tier I FBA

We begin with a Tier 1 FBA. The K-5 elementary school in this case example is located in a suburban area and has an enrollment of almost 600 students with a free and reduced lunch rate of about 25%. Data that the team will review is from the 2009–2010 academic year. The 2010–2011 school year has just begun, and the team is reviewing the data from the previous year to evaluate progress with the implementation of school-wide interventions. The individual details for Samuel will not be apparent until Tier 2 and Tier 3, but this example illustrates how his case emerged from an analysis of school-wide data.

Reviewing School-wide Data

The team began by reviewing the Big Six ODR data at their first meeting of the year to determine if there is a problem and what the setting events/antecedents, behaviors, and consequences are in the school. They will then use these data to develop a precision hypothesis statement that will be used to develop action plans to improve school behavior.

Average Referrals per Day per Month

As noted in Chapter 3, a graph of average referrals per day per month is a summary of the general level of problem behavior in a school over time. It can be used to answer the basic question, "Do we have a problem?" by comparing levels of ODRs over time (i.e., Is there a recent increase in referrals?) or by comparing school ODR levels to the national norms (i.e., Does our school have more referrals than would be expected in comparable schools?). The 2009–2010 ODR data for major referrals (not minor referrals) indicate that K–6 schools average 0.22 referrals per 100 students per day. So, this K–5 school with 600 students in 2009–2010 would be expected to have 1.32 referrals every day. The team decided that if the referrals were above the national norms, then they would review current behavior trends and Tier 1 interventions to address those behaviors. The graph for this elementary school's referrals per day per month is provided in Figure 8.1. This graph indicates that ODRs occurred at a rate of 1.5 per day in November, February, March, April, and May, with the largest spike in March. The team decided that this is a problem that needs to be defined in more detail by reviewing the remaining Big Six data.

Referrals by Problem Behavior

A graph that depicts referrals by problem behavior informs the school team as to which behaviors represent the biggest problem in the school, thereby

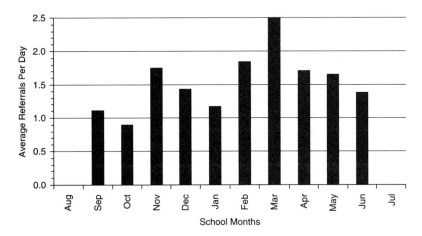

FIGURE 8.1 Elementary school's graph of average referrals per day per month from case example. Graph generated using the School-Wide Information System (www.swis.org).

clarifying the behavior in the setting event/antecedent, behavior, consequence model at Tier 1. The team reviewed the graph presented in Figure 8.2, which indicates that the most commonly occurring problem behaviors in the elementary school are disruption, physical aggression, and disrespect during the 2009–2010 academic year.

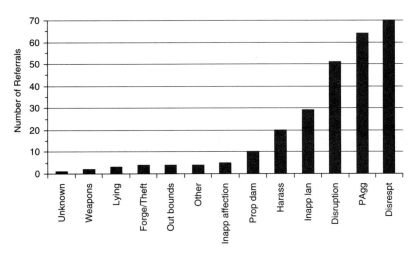

FIGURE 8.2 Elementary school's graph of referrals by problem behavior from case example. Graph generated using the School-Wide Information System (www.swis.org).

Functional Behavioral Assessment

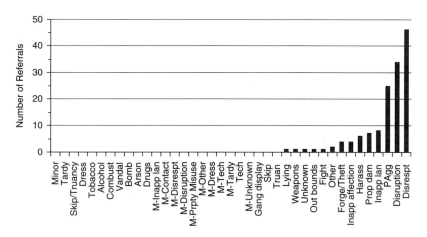

FIGURE 8.3 Elementary school's graph of referrals by problem behavior for grades K–1 from case example. Graph generated using the School-Wide Information System (www.swis.org).

Teams may elect to break down data by grade, teachers within a grade, or any subset that may provide the team with more detailed information to best address the areas of concern. In this case example, the team was interested in looking at grade-specific data to see if the problem behavior differed by grade. The team created a custom graph using School-Wide Information System (SWIS; May et al., 2010) to identify the problem behavior for grades K–1 (see Figure 8.3), grades 2–3 (see Figure 8.4), and grades 4–5 (see Figure 8.5).

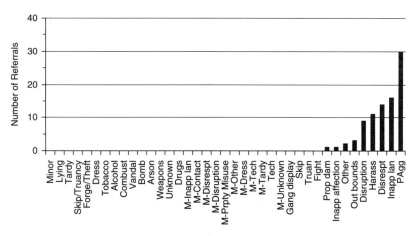

FIGURE 8.4 Elementary school's graph of referrals by problem behavior for grades 2–3 from case example. Graph generated using the School-Wide Information System (www.swis.org).

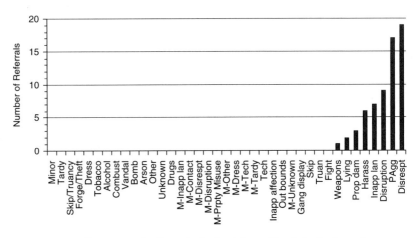

FIGURE 8.5 Elementary school's graph of referrals by problem behavior for grades 4–5 from case example. Graph generated using the School-Wide Information System (www.swis.org).

They noted that, although disrespect and disruption were the main ODRs in kindergarten through first grade, physical aggression was the primary ODR problem in second and third grades, and disrespect and physical aggression were the primary ODR problems in fourth and fifth grades.

The team also noticed that the number of referrals appeared to decrease after first grade. They decided to compare the data for each of the problem behaviors and graph it to see if there was an increase or decrease as the students moved from kindergarten to fifth grade (see Figures 8.6–8.8).

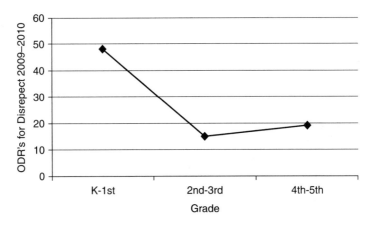

FIGURE 8.6 Elementary school's graph of office discipline referrals (ODRs) for disrespect by grade from case example.

Functional Behavioral Assessment

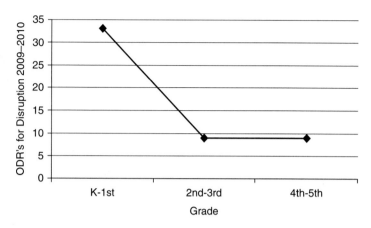

FIGURE 8.7 Elementary school's graph office discipline referrals (ODRs) for disruption by grade from case example.

By reviewing these data, the team discovered that the ODRs for kindergarten to first grade were significantly higher in the areas of disrespect and disruption, and the number of ODRs in these areas dropped for second through third grades and fourth and fifth grades. However, ODRs were higher for kindergarten to first grade, and increased a bit more in second and third grades for physical aggression. In fourth and fifth grades, the ODRs for physical aggression decreased; however, it was still occurring at a problematic level. The team concluded that interventions to address disrespect and disruption should be targeted to K–1 and interventions to address physical aggression should be targeted at K–5.

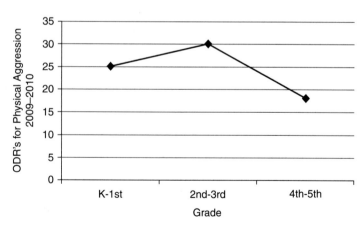

FIGURE 8.8 Elementary school's graph of office discipline referrals (ODRs) for physical aggression by grade from case example.

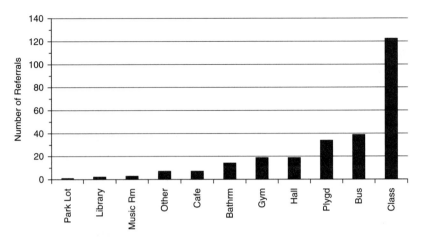

FIGURE 8.9 Elementary school's graph of referrals by location from case example. Graph generated using the School-Wide Information System (www.swis.org).

Referrals by Location

The locations in which behavioral violations occur provide good antecedent information. When the team reviewed Figure 8.9, it appeared that a large number of ODRs were coming from a specific location, the classroom. The team deduced that there was something about that setting that was triggering or facilitating problem behavior. As a general rule of thumb, students would be expected to spend around 60% of their day in the classroom; so if less than 60% of the referrals are coming from the classroom, then this might not imply that the classroom was the most significant predictor of problem behavior. In this elementary case, more than 50% of referrals were coming from the classroom, and there was no clear pattern of any other location being strongly represented in the data. Therefore, the team determined that the classroom was the best location predictor of problem behavior in the school.

Referrals by Time

Determining the time of day during which behavioral violations occur can provide more clarity to the antecedents to problem behavior. As was the case with referrals by location, this information does not necessarily explain what it is about this antecedent that is directly and functionally related to the behavior. However, it can be the basis for reasonable hypotheses. The team review of Figure 8.10 revealed ODRs occurred at a rate of five or more per

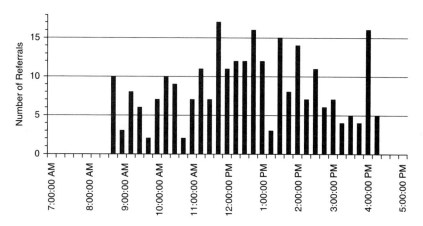

FIGURE 8.10 Elementary school's graph of referrals by time from case example. Graph generated using the School-Wide Information System (www.swis.org).

hour throughout most of the day, with few times below that level. There was never 1 full hour of time in which there were consistently fewer than five referrals. Therefore, there was no apparent pattern in the referrals by time on which the team focused as a strength or a concern.

Referrals by Student

One of the important questions to ask when using school-wide ODR data to conduct an FBA of student behavior is whether the problem is better explained as being pervasive and school-wide, or if the problems in school are better understood as being the result of the problem behaviors of a small group of students. If the problem is a small group of students rather than a situation in which many students have just a few referrals, then the focus would shift from analyzing and changing antecedents and consequences in the whole school to conducting individual student Tier 2 FBAs and providing FBA-based interventions for these specific students. In reviewing Figure 8.11, the team discussed the fact that it would be beneficial to determine exactly how many students had one ODR, how many had two to five ODRs, and how many had six or more ODRs, so that they could plan for supports across the tiers. To accomplish this, they created a special table from their data that indicated that about 20% of students had received at least one ODR in that past year. They also noted that about 9% had received two or more ODRs in the same period. The team is aware that students with two or more ODRs in 2009–2010 should be considered for Tier 2 or 3 interventions and therefore

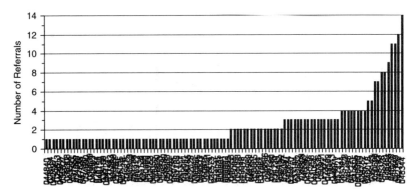

FIGURE 8.11 Elementary school's graph of referrals by students from case example. The tightly clustered text along the *x*-axis is the students' identification numbers. Graph generated using the School-Wide Information System (www.swis.org).

conducted Tier 2 FBAs for those students after the action plan was developed and implemented for Tier 1 supports. The Tier 2 FBA process for this case example is described in a later section in this chapter.

Referrals by Motivation for Most Frequent Problem Behavior

ODR information is most useful to an FBA process when it includes information about the motivation/consequences of behaviors that are referred, thus completing the setting event/antecedent, behavior, consequence model of FBA. Therefore, the team reviewed this sixth graph (or, in this case, a series

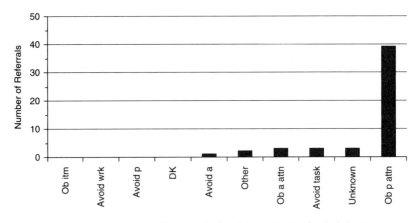

FIGURE 8.12 Elementary school's graph of referrals by motivation for the behavior of disruption from case example. Graph generated using the School-Wide Information System (www.swis.org).

Functional Behavioral Assessment

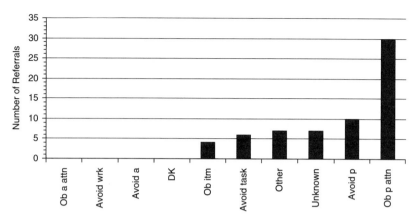

FIGURE 8.13 Elementary school's graph of referrals by motivation for the behavior of physical aggression from case example. Graph generated using the School-Wide Information System (www.swis.org).

of graphs). For this case example, a motivation graph has been developed for each of the three most prevalent problem behaviors: disruption, physical aggression, and disrespect (see Figures 8.12–8.14). The team noted that, although disrespectful behavior appears to be motivated by "avoid task," both physical aggression and disruption appeared to be motivated by "obtain peer attention." Therefore, the team noted that for students in K–1, where the primary ODR was disrespect, the task avoidance function must be addressed. For students in K–1, where the next prevalent ODR is for disruption, and

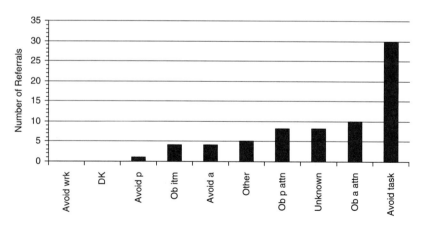

FIGURE 8.14 Elementary school's graph of referrals by motivation for the behavior of disrespect from case example. Graph generated using the School-Wide Information System (www.swis.org).

in second and third grades, where the hypothesized function was obtain peer attention, an intervention that addresses the peer attention function was considered. Additionally, the team determined that the interventions should be delivered in the classrooms, which is the primary location of the ODRs.

Summarizing Tier 1 Functional Behavioral Assessment Data: Precision Hypothesis Statements

After reviewing the Big Six ODR data for Tier 1 FBAs, the team developed a precision hypothesis statement, which is a precise definition of the problem

Developing Tier 1 FBA Precision Hypothesis Statements

Behavior	Students	Location/Time of Day	Motivation	Precision Statement
Disruption	More likely to occur in grades K-1st	Classroom	Obtain Peer Attention	1. During the 2009–10 academic year there were 73 ODRs from the classroom for disruption. The problem behavior occurs in more than 40% of the student population (2+ referrals) indicating the problem is school-wide. There is no clear pattern indicating that the month or the time of day predicts the problem behavior. However, it is more likely to occur in grades K-1st and appears to be motivated by obtaining peer attention.
Physical Aggression	More likely to occur K-5th	Classroom	Obtain Peer Attention	2. During the 2009–10 academic year there were 52 ODRs from the classroom for physical aggression. The problem behavior occurs in more than 40% of the student population (2+ referrals) indicating the problem is school-wide. There is no clear pattern indicating that the month or the time of day predicts the problem behavior. However, it is more likely to occur in grades K-5th and appears to be motivated by avoiding a task.
Disrespect	More likely to occur K-1st	Classroom	Avoid Task	3. During the 2009–10 academic year there were 73 ODRs from the classroom for disrespect. The problem behavior occurs in more than 40% of the student population (2+ referrals) indicating the problem is school-wide. There is no clear pattern indicating that the month or the time of day predicts the problem behavior. However, it is more likely to occur in grades K-1st stand appears to be motivated by avoiding a task.

FIGURE 8.15 Elementary school case example Tier 1 functional behavioral assessment (FBA) precision hypothesis statements.

Functional Behavioral Assessment

behavior that also describes the setting events, antecedents, and consequences. The team began by separately summarizing the information from the Big Six. This information was then combined into a precision hypothesis statement, a comprehensive statement about how the setting events, antecedents, behaviors, and consequences relate to one another. The team developed three precision hypotheses statements to match the three behaviors and related functions (see Figure 8.15).

Developing Interventions and Action Planning with Goals and Decisions

By clearly identifying the setting events/antecedents, behaviors, and consequences in a precision hypothesis statement, a team is able to identify variables in the school that could be changed in Tier 1, in order to change student behavior and develop efficient and logical interventions, as illustrated in Figure 8.16.

After Tier 1 FBA-based interventions were developed, the team documented the intervention details, a plan to measure the effects of the intervention, and data-based decisions about the intervention's continued use on an action planning form (see Figure 8.17). This action planning document is used in every meeting and is organized around intervention decisions. This ensures that intervention ideas developed several meetings ago do not get lost in the paperwork shuffle between meetings, and it promotes accountability for the team. In this case, the team developed measurable goals based on ODRs for each of the three interventions that will help them decide if the

Tier 1 Behavior Problem	Logical and Efficient Tier 1 Intervention
Disrespect in the classroom motivated by escape from task (with emphasis on K-1st)	Re-teach respect to all K-1 students and implement Good Behavior Game in classrooms (Tingstrom, Sterling-Turner, & Wilczynski, 2006)
Disruptive behaviors in the classroom motivated by obtain peer attention (with emphasis on K-1st)	Develop a positive peer reporting system in K-1 classrooms wherein students acknowledge one another's positive behavior (Skinner, Neddenriep, Robinson, Ervin, & Jones, 2002)
Physical aggression in the classroom motivated by obtaining peer attention	Develop a positive peer reporting system in all classrooms and develop an inter-class time out procedure for aggression (Nelson & Carr, 1996; Skinner et al., 2002)

FIGURE 8.16 Intervention ideas for Tier 1 behavior problems from case example.

Tier 1 FBA-Based Action Planning

Activity	Expected Outcome	Person Responsible	Begin Date	Review Date	Decision (continue, eliminate, modify)
1. Re-teach respect to all K-1 students and implement Good Behavior Game in classrooms	The team expects to see a 50% reduction in ODRs for disrespect in the K-1 classrooms within 2 months	Arleen	10/1	12/1	
2. Implement a positive peer reporting system in all classrooms wherein students acknowledge one another's positive behavior	The team expects to see a 50% reduction in ODRs for disruptive behavior in the classroom within 2 months.	Marcy	10/1	12/1	
3. Implement an inter-class time out procedure for aggression wherein students are re-directed when showing signs of physical aggression and sent to a partner classroom (Use the Think Time Strategy by Nelson & Carr, 1996).	The team expects to see a 50% reduction in ODRs for physical aggression in the classroom within 2 months	Tony	10/1	12/1	

FIGURE 8.17 Tier 1 action plan for implementing and monitoring functional behavioral assessment (FBA)-based interventions from case example.

interventions are effective. As the team began implementing these school-wide interventions, they also turned their attention to the students in need of Tier 2 FBA supports, as described below.

Tier 2 Functional Behavioral Assessment

The team began the Tier 2 FBA process by determining which students had two to five ODRs, using the graph in Figure 8.18. A Tier 2 FBA was

Functional Behavioral Assessment

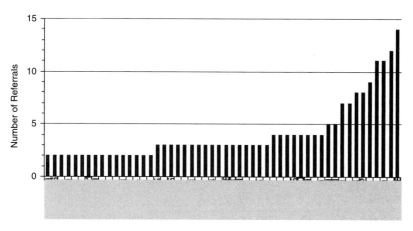

FIGURE 8.18 Elementary school's graph of referrals for students with two or more referrals from case example. The text along the x-axis is the students' identification numbers. Graph generated using the School-Wide Information System (www.swis.org).

conducted for each of these students, which included a review of the existing ODR data, a record review, and a brief interview. They were then matched to evidenced-based packaged interventions. To illustrate this process, this case example focuses on a first-grade student named Samuel, who was in kindergarten during the 2009–2010 school year and had four ODRs that year.

Functional Behavioral Assessment Data Collection
The first step in Samuel's case was for the team to review the summary of his ODR data (see Figure 8.19), keeping in mind that these data are from the previous school year, in which Samuel attended half-day kindergarten; he is now attending school full days. These data indicated that his most common problem behavior was physical aggression toward peers, half of the behaviors occurred in the classroom and half of them occurred on the school bus, and the most common motivation was to obtain peer attention.

Following the examination of ODR data, the team identified one team member, the school social worker, to take the lead in reviewing Samuel's educational records and conducting a brief FBA interview. The review of the records is a quick analysis of the student's archival data that can inform interventions. Information was reviewed for Samuel's strengths and for patterns that interfere with his school success, such as high mobility between schools, frequent changes of address, series of excused or unexcused absences, grades, and health records, including visits to the school nurse. Any information that

Date	Grade	Staff	Time	Location	Problem Behavior	Motivation	Others Involved	Admin Decision
5/10/10 spit on student who he thought pushed him	K	Teacher A	10:00 AM	Class	Other	Other	Peers	Office
2/14/10 Hit student on bus	K	Bus Driver	11:45 AM	Bus	Physical Aggression	Obtain Peer Attention	Peers	Confe-rence
2/10/10 Threw block at another student	K	Teacher A	9:30 AM	Class	Physical Aggression	Obtain peer attention	Peers	Office
10/4/2009	K	Bus Driver	9:00 AM	Bus	M-Disruption	Obtain peer attention	None	Conf

FIGURE 8.19 Summary of Samuel's office discipline referrals (ODRs) from 2009 to 2010. Graph generated using the School-Wide Information System (www.swis.org) and modified to protect confidential information.

STUDENT RECORDS REVIEW

Name of Student: ___**Samuel Johnson**_____ Grade___**1**_____

Attendance (e.g., excused and unexcused absences, number of schools attended)

Number of days absent:

PK____ K_**2**_ 1st ____ 2nd ____ 3rd ____ 4th ____ 5th ____ 6th ____ 7th ____

8th ____ 9th ____ 10th ____ 11th ____ 12th ____

Strengths/Patterns: **Student attended school regularly.**

Health (e.g., frequency of visits to school nurse, medical history, medications)
PK____ K_**1**_ 1st ____ 2nd ____ 3rd ____ 4th ____ 5th ____ 6th ____ 7th ____

8th ____ 9th ____ 10th ____ 11th ____ 12th ____

Strengths/Patterns: **There is no pattern of school nurse visits beyond normal expectations for students. Records indicate that student is not taking medications at school and has no remarkable medical history that could impact behavior.**

Academics (e.g., grades, standardized test scores)

Strengths/Patterns: Student's grades were all satisfactory "S" for the school year.

There was no indication of additional behavior issues in the classroom.

Social/Emotional (e.g. current stressors, information about previous behavior problems)

Strengths/Patterns: **Records indicate that the only evidence of a life stressor is the transition to Kindergarten with no history of attending preschool or daycare. The team should take into consideration that the 1st grade year will also be a transition from a ½ day educational setting to a full day.**

FIGURE 8.20 Samuel's completed Tier 2 record review.

might indicate antecedents or functions of behavior and/or support preliminary hypotheses regarding the function of behavior would be important to present to the team. The findings from the record review are presented in Figure 8.20. The social worker noted in the records that Samuel did not attend a preschool or daycare. Therefore, kindergarten was his first experience in a more structured setting, and riding a bus was still a relatively new experience.

A brief FBA interview was conducted with Samuel's first-grade teacher. Since half of the ODRs from the previous academic year occurred on the bus and half in the classroom, the team felt that the teacher might be able to provide the most accurate information possible for a brief FBA interview. The Tier 2 FBA interview is largely unstructured and took about 10 minutes to complete. The social worker asked the teacher about the setting events, antecedents, and consequences for the problem behavior. The interview was very

Brief FBA Interview

Name of student: **Samuel Johnson**   Date **September 25, 2010**
Name of Interviewer: **Michelle Alvarez** Name of Person Interviewed: **Mr. Hernandez-1st grade Teacher**

Antecedent
Transitions between instructional activities

Behavior
Student hits other students as he moves between activities
Student moves chair out in front of other students
Student sits too close to other students

Consequence
Peers say something negative about other student
Peers tell teacher what other student has done
Teacher asks student to not hit other students as they move around the classroom
Teacher asks student to move chair carefully so that it is not in the way of other students
Teacher reminds student what personal space is and asks student not to sit too close to other students

Setting Event (if possible)

Additional notes
Teacher is concerned about student's social skills with peers. She said that although she has not contacted parent as of this date she will be calling parent within this next week. Teacher also shared she learned from student that there are no children his age in his neighborhood and he is an only child. She said that he shared with her that aside from school he has no one to play with.

Summary Statement

Setting Event/Antecedent	Behavior	Maintaining Consequence
Transition between activity	**Physical Aggression**	**Obtain peer attention**

FIGURE 8.21 Brief functional behavioral assessment (FBA) interview with Samuel's classroom teacher.

informal and provided the team with enough information to inform a tentative precision hypothesis statement that it used when matching the function of student behavior to evidence-based package interventions.

The results of the interview indicated that Samuel continues to exhibit physical aggression in class this year, to the point that his teacher is going to contact his parents within the next week (Figure 8.21). In response to these disruptions, the other students tell the teacher about what the student is doing and the teacher tries to redirect Samuel to use more appropriate behavior. The information gathered in the brief interview and information from the ODR data and records review led the team to the development of a precision hypothesis statement. The process for developing a precision hypothesis statement is described in the next section.

Summarizing Functional Behavioral Assessment Information into a Precision Hypothesis Statement

After considering the data gathered in the Tier 2 FBA, the team decided on the following precision hypothesis statement for Samuel:

> Based on interviews, ODR data, records review, and brief teacher interview, it appears that *physical aggression* is most likely to occur when *the student transitions between activities* and is maintained by *obtaining peer attention*.

Tier 2 Interventions

The team evaluated their list of effective and efficient Tier 2 package interventions in the school prior to this process (see Figure 8.22). The team was then able to consult their list of Tier 2 interventions and select the intervention that best matched the function of Samuel's behavior.

Samuel was referred for participation in the Social Skills Improvement System (see Elliott & Gresham, 2008) group that was scheduled to begin 2 weeks later. By that time, the remaining students referred for Tier 2 FBAs were reviewed, and recommendations were made for the most appropriate intervention matched to their behavior function. Also during this time, baseline data were collected for each student. The Social Skills Improvement System group had seven students in it. The progress of each student was monitored in a small group format (see Figure 8.23) to ensure that students

Evaluating Tier 2 Interventions in School

Intervention	Evaluation					
	Evidence-based?	Function addressed	Non-responder decision rule?	Implementation fidelity assessed?	Effective?	Decision
Social Skills Improvement System (Elliott & Gresham, 2008)	(Y)/N	Attention Escape (Both)	(Y) N	(Y) N	(Y)N	E (M*) **Will implement and measure fidelity for first time in fall 10**
Check in/ Check out (Crone, Horner, & Hawken, 2004)	Y/N	(Attention) Escape Both	(Y) N	(Y) N	(Y)N	E (M*)
Individual meetings with assistant principal	Y/(N)	Attention ?Escape Both	Y (N)	Y/(N)	Y/(N)	(E) M

*E = eliminate; M = maintain

FIGURE 8.22 Tier 2 intervention evaluation from Samuel's school. Adapted with permission from PBIS Training Manual (www.pbis.org).

were responding to the intervention and that the intervention was being implemented with fidelity. Samuel's data were collected using daily direct behavior ratings (DBRs) by his teacher. His graphed data indicated that he was not making improvement while in the Social Skills Improvement System group (see Figure 8.24). Therefore, the team decided to place Samuel in the Check In/Check Out program (see Crone, Horner, & Hawken, 2004) in the school and updated the group tracking form to indicate this (see Figure 8.23). This intervention led to a slight decrease in behavior (see Figure 8.24), but the team felt that Samuel's data indicated that more intensive, Tier 3 supports would be necessary to support his behavior. Therefore, the team referred Samuel for a Tier 3 FBA and discontinued his involvement in Check

Tier 2 FBA Tracking and Process Form

Students/ Grade/Home-room Teacher	Date Brief FBA Competed	Hypothesized Function	Intervention Selected	Begin Date	End Date	Decision (different Tier 2 intervention, move to Tier 1, move to Tier 3)
1. Samuel Johnson/ 1st Grade/ Hernandez	9/25/10	Obtain Peer Attention	Social Skills Improvement System	10/10/10	12/15/10	Different Tier 2 interv
			Check in/ Check out	12/19/10	2/5/11	Move to Tier 3
2. Aiden Milfor/ 3rd Grade/ Jameson	10/1/10	Escape Difficult Tasks	Modified Check in/ Check out	10/19/10		
3. Mya Tillman/ 2nd Grade	10/5/10	Obtain Peer Attention	Social Skills Improvement System	10/10/10		
4.						

FIGURE 8.23 Team tracking form for students referred to Tier 2 interventions in Samuel's school.

In/Check Out after an individualized FBA-based behavior intervention plan (FBA-BIP) was implemented.

Tier 3 Functional Behavioral Assessment
Data Collection

After the team decided that Samuel would require more intensive Tier 3 supports, they met to review the findings from Tiers 1 and 2 and determine who would complete the interviews and observations for the Tier 3 FBA. The FBA findings from Tiers 1 and 2, which included Samuel's ODRs, a review of his school records, and a brief interview with his classroom teacher indicated

Functional Behavioral Assessment

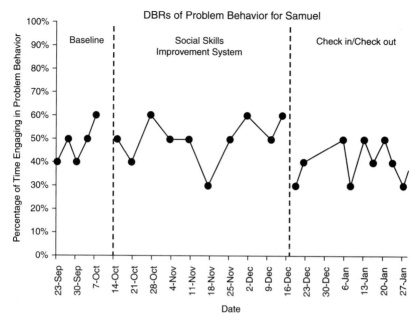

FIGURE 8.24 Graph of direct behavior rating (DBR0 data for two interventions implemented at Tier 2 for Samuel.

that Samuel engaged in physical aggression during transitions between activities. The attempts to improve his behavior at Tier 2 included two package interventions, neither of which led to a significant improvement in his behavior. The team then decided that it would need higher-quality information about the setting events, antecedents, and consequences of his behavior to plan an individualized FBA-BIP.

The team decided that the school social worker would conduct the interviews and the school psychologist would conduct the observations. The interviews were conducted with Samuel's regular classroom teacher, his music teacher, and his mother. The Functional Assessment Checklist for Teachers and Staff (FACTS; March et al., 2000) was used for the interviews with teachers. The results of the classroom teacher interview are presented in Figure 8.25. The hypothesis from this interview was that physical aggression and verbally inappropriate behavior were occasioned by negative social interactions during boring tasks and were maintained by escape from peer attention. It is interesting to note that this differs from the original brief FBA interview with the same teacher from Tier 2, which indicated that the behavior was maintained by obtaining peer attention. The results of the interviews with

---

Functional Assessment Checklist for Teachers and Staff (FACTS-Part A)

Step 1 Student/Grade: __**Samuel**__   Date: __**2-15-11**__
Interviewer: __**Arleen**__   Respondent(s): __**Mr. Hernandez**__

Step 2 **Student Profile:** Please identify at least three strengths or contributions the student brings to school.
__**Samuel likes to help others, tries hard with his school work, and is always on**__
__**time**__

Step 3 **Problem Behavior(s): Identify problem behaviors**

___ Tardy	__X__ Fight/physical Aggression	___ Disruptive	___ Theft
___ Unresponsive	___ Inappropriate Language	___ Insubordination	___ Vandalism
___ Withdrawn	__X__ Verbal Harassment	___ Work not done	___ Other _____
	__X__ Verbally Inappropriate	___ Self-injury	

Describe problem behavior: _____

Step 4 **Identifying Routines: Where, When and With Whom Problem Behaviros are Most Likely.**

Schedule (Times)	Activity	Likelihood of Problem Behavior	Specific Problem Behavior
9:15	Math	Low 1 2 ③ 4 5 High 6	**Verbally Inappropriate**
9:45	Reading	1 2 3 ④ 5 6	**Phys Aggression**
10:30	Writing/Spelling	1 ② 3 4 5 6	**None**
11:00	Art	1 2 3 4 ⑤ 6	**Verbal Harass/Inapp**
11:30	Lunch/Recess	1 2 3 ④ 5 6	**Phys Aggression**
12:10	Group Reading	1 2 3 4 5 ⑥	**Phys Aggression/Verbal**
12:45	Group Math	1 2 3 4 ⑤ 6	**Phys Aggression/Verbal**
1:30	Music/P.E.	1 2 3 ④ 5 6	**Verbal Aggression**
2:15	Activity Time	1 2 3 ④ 5 6	**Verbal Aggression**
2:45	Dismiss	1 2 3 ④ 5 6	**Phys Aggression**
		1 2 3 4 5 6	

Step 5 **Select 1-3 Routines for further assessment: Select routines based on (a) similarity of activities (conditions) with ratings of 4, 5 or 6 and (b) similarity of problem behaviro(s). Complete the FACTS-Part B for each routine identified.**

March, Horner, Lewis-Palmer, Brown, Crone, Todd & Carr (2000)

FIGURE 8.25 Completed Functional Assessment Checklist for Teachers and Staff (FACTS) interview with classroom teacher for Samuel.

Functional Assessment Checklist for Teachers & Staff (FACTS-Part B)

Step 1
Student/Grade: _____ Date: _____

Interviewer: _____ Respondent(s): _____

Step 2
Routine/Activities/Context: Which routine (only one) from the FACTS-Part A is assessed?

Routine/Activities/Context:	Problem Behavior(s)
Group Reading and Group Math	Physical Aggression and Verbally Inappropriate

Step 3
Provide more detail about the problem behavior(s):

What does the problem behavior(s) look like? **Verbal = Saying naughty words**
Physical = Hitting other kids with hands

How often does the problem behavior(s) occur? **Verbal = 5x/class period**
Physical = 2 or 3x/week

How long does the problem behavior(s) last when it does occur? **Verbal = 10 seconds**
Physical = 2 seconds

What is the intensity/level of danger of the problem behavior(s)? **Verbal = low**
Physical = moderate (no marks)

Step 4
What are the events that predict when the problem behavior(s) will occur? (Predictors)

Related Issues (setting events)		Environmental Features	
___ illness Other:_____		___ reprimand/correction	___ structured activity
___ drug use _____		___ physical demands	**X** unstructured time
X negative social _____		___ socially isolated	**X** tasks too boring
___ conflict at home _____		**X** with peers	___ activity too long
___ academic failure _____		___ Other	___ tasks too difficult

Step 5
What consequences appear most likely to maintain the problem behavior(s)?

Things that are Obtained		Things Avoided or Escaped From	
___ adult attention Other:_____		___ hard tasks Other: _____	
X peer attention _____		___ reprimands _____	
___ preferred activity _____		**X** peer negatives _____	
___ money/things _____		___ physical effort _____	
		___ adult attention _____	

SUMMARY OF BEHAVIOR
Identify the summary that will be used to build a plan of behavior support.

Step 6

Setting Events & Predictors	Problem Behavior(s)	Maintaining Consequence(s)
Negative social interactions with peers during boring tasks	Physical aggression and verbally inappropriate	Escape from peer attention

Step 7
How confident are you that the <u>Summary of Behavior</u> is accurate?

Not very confident .... Very Confident
1 .... 2 .... 3 .... 4 .... (5) 6

Step 8
What current efforts have been used to control the problem behavior?

Strategies for preventing problem behavior		Strategies for responding to problem behavior	
___ schedule change Other: _____		**X** reprimand Other: _____	
___ seating change **Restating expectations**		**X** office referral _____	
___ curriculum change _____		___ detention _____	

March, Horner, Lewis-Palmer, Brown, Crone, Todd & Carr (2000)

FIGURE 8.25 Continued.

the music teacher using the FACTS interview indicated that the primary problem behavior was verbal aggression and that it was occasioned by group musical activities and maintained by escape from peer attention. The brief FBA interview with Samuel's mother indicated that the most common problem behavior at home was yelling at and hitting his siblings. She indicated that it occurred most often when his siblings were playing with a toy he wanted or being mean to him, and was maintained by obtaining the toy or escaping the sibling interaction.

After the interviews were complete, the school psychologist conducted the observations using the Functional Behavioral Assessment Observation

FBA OBSERVATION AND SUMMARY FORM (FBA-OSF)

STUDENT: __Samuel__   OBSERVER: __Andrew__

BEHAVIOR INCIDENT #	Physical aggression	Inappropriate language	DIFFICULT	EASY	LONG	SEATWORK	TEACHER-LED INSTRUCTION	UNSTRUCTURED TIME	WITH ADULT	WITH PEER(S)	ALONE/NO ATTENTION	OBTAIN: ADULT ATTENTION	OBTAIN: PEER ATTENTION	OBTAIN: TASK/ACTIVITY	OBTAIN: TANGIBLE	AVOID: ADULT ATTENTION	AVOID: PEER ATTENTION	AVOID: TASK/ACTIVITY	AVOID: TANGIBLE	Reading Group	Math Group	DATE: February 21st	DATE: February 22nd	DATE:
1		X					X			X							X			X		12:12		
2		X					X			X							X			X		12:20		
3	X						X			X		X								X		12:26		
4		X				X				X							X			X		12:40		
5	X						X			X							X				X	12:48		
6		X					X			X						X					X	12:59		
7		X				X				X							X				X	1:15		
8		X				X				X							X			X			12:20	
9		X					X			X			X							X			12:27	
10		X				X				X							X			X			12:38	
11		X				X				X							X			X			12:41	
12		X				X				X							X				X		12:55	
13	X						X			X						X					X		1:15	
14		X				X				X							X				X		1:28	
15																								
TOTAL	3	11				7	7			14		1	1			2	10			8	6			

RESPONSE CLASS #1

ANTECEDENT	BEHAVIOR	CONSEQUENCE
Group work with peers	Inappropriate Language and Physical aggression	Escape peer attention

RESPONSE CLASS #2

ANTECEDENT	BEHAVIOR	CONSEQUENCE

FIGURE 8.26 Completed Functional Behavioral Assessment Observation Summary Form (FBA-OSF) observation for Samuel.

Summary Form (FBA-OSF). Based on the results from the interviews, he determined that it would be best to observe physical aggression and verbally inappropriate behavior during group reading and group math time since that is when these problem behaviors were most likely to occur. After 2 days of observations in each activity, 14 incidents of the behaviors were observed and appeared to be occasioned by group work with peers (seatwork and teacher-led instruction) and maintained by escape from peer attention (see Figure 8.26).

Precision Hypothesis Statement

After carefully reviewing the findings of all data sources from Tiers 1, 2, and 3, the team noted that the early hypotheses focused on the function of obtaining peer attention, whereas the latter and more reliable data suggested a function of escape from peer attention. It was decided that the latter hypothesis was more accurate and that the Tier 1 and Tier 2 data may have been inaccurate because of the lack of rigor in the data collection process at those levels. For example, the perceived motivation on the ODRs may have been inaccurate because the referring staff simply noted that peers had been involved and then made the assumption that Samuel was trying to get their attention. The team noticed that the data at Tier 3 were fairly consistent in the setting events, antecedents, behaviors, and consequences that they suggested. Therefore, the team developed the following precision hypothesis statement, based primarily on the Tier 3 FBA data:

> Based on multiple interviews, direct observations in the classroom, ODR data, and a records review, it appears that *physical aggression and inappropriate verbal behavior* are most likely to occur after *negative peer interactions* and are maintained by *escaping peer attention*. This whole sequence often occurs in the context of *group work (reading and math)*.

Intervention Planning and Implementation

Before writing the FBA-BIP, the team brainstormed interventions that matched the setting events, antecedents, behaviors, and consequences in the precision hypothesis statement using the form in Figure 8.27. The team then developed

	SETTING EVENT(S)	ANTECEDENT(S)	BEHAVIOR(S)	CONSEQUENCE(S)
FBA SUMMARY	Group work with peers	Negative peer interactions	Verbally inappropriate and physical aggression	Escape peer attention
POSSIBLE INTERVENTIONS	SETTING EVENT MANIPULATIONS • Non-contingent escape • Have adult supervise all group work • Eliminate group work	ANTECEDENT MANIPULATIONS • Teach other students to not antagonize Samuel • Remind Samuel to walk away from verbal fights before each group activity	BEHAVIOR MANIPULATIONS • Teach Samuel to walk away from conflict • Remind students how to be respectful in the classroom • Teach Samuel to recognize signs that he is getting angry	CONSEQUENCE MANIPULATIONS • Allow Samuel to skip last 10 minutes of group work if no behaviors occur during group work • Require Samuel to apologize to classmates after aggression

FIGURE 8.27 Possible interventions matched the setting events, antecedents, behaviors, and consequences in the case of Samuel.

a comprehensive FBA-BIP by selecting the most effective and contextually appropriate interventions from the brainstormed list and developing short- and long-term goals (see Figure 8.28). The fidelity of the FBA-BIP was monitored by the school social worker using a checklist of the features of the interventions in the plan. The first fidelity check indicated that one component of the plan was not being implemented well, and an item was added to the action plan at the end the form (see page five of Figure 8.28). The effects of the intervention were monitored by the classroom teacher using daily DBRs. The school psychologist gathered these data and graphed it weekly on the fourth page of the FBA-BIP form. The data indicated that the short-term goal of a 50% reduction was nearly met, and the latter data indicated a continuing downward trend in physical aggression and verbally inappropriate behavior. The team was therefore optimistic that the long-term goal would be met.

In the future, the team will continue to monitor fidelity and outcomes and will meet to action plan around any changes that should be made to meet the long-term goal. It is hoped that Samuel's FBA-BIP can be faded after the long-term goal is met and that his behavior can be supported with less-intensive Tier 2 or Tier 1 interventions.

FBA-BASED BEHAVIOR INTERVENTION PLAN (FBA-BIP)

STUDENT NAME ___**Samuel**_____

TEAM MEMBERS ___**Arleen, Andrew, Hector, and Carol**_____

SUMMARY OF FBA

FBA COMPLETION DATE ___**3/1/2011**_____

DATA COLLECTORS ___**Arleen and Andrew**_____

SOURCES OF DATA

RECORD REVIEW ☒   TEACHER INTERVIEW(S) ☒   GUARDIAN INTERVIEW(S) ☒
STUDENT INTEREVIEW ☐ DIRECT OBSERVATION ☒   OTHER ☐ _____

	SETTING EVENT(S)	ANTECEDENT(S)	BEHAVIOR(S)	CONSEQUENCE(S)
FBA SUMMARY	**Group work with peers** →	**Negative peer interactions** →	**Verbally inappropriate and physical aggression** →	**Escape peer attention**

FIGURE 8.28 The functional behavioral assessment-based behavior intervention plan (FBA-BIP) for Samuel.

BEHAVIOR INTERVENTION PLAN

	INTERVENTION	DETAILED DESCRIPTION OF INTERVENTION	IMPLEMENTER(S)
SETTING EVENT MANIPULATION	Adult supervision for group work	The teacher or another adult in the classroom will use proximity management and closely monitor any peer group that Samuel is working with during the day.	Hector
ANTECEDENT MANIPULATION	Prompt appropriate behavior	Before each group activity, the teacher will remind Samuel to walk away from any disputes with his classmates.	Hector
BEHAVIOR MANIPULATION	Teach Samuel to walk away from disputes	The social worker will teacher teach Samuel how to recognize when he is getting angry and to walk away whenever a dispute begins with a classmate	Arleen
CONSEQUENCE MANIPULATION	Escape group work if behavior is good (DRO)	If Samuel does not display any problem behavior during group work, then he will be allowed to escape the last 10 minutes of group and engage in a preferred activity	Hector
OTHER (DESCRIBE) Consequence	Restorative measures for problem behavior	Whenever Samuel displays aggression against a peer, he will be required to apologize to that student and help her/him with homework for at least 10 minutes. This will ensure that he doesn't escape the peer interaction when he is aggressive.	Hector

FIGURE 8.28 Continued.

EVALUATION PLAN

<u>FIDELITY OF IMPLEMENTATION</u>

PERSON RESPONSIBLE FOR EVALUATION   <u>**Arleen**</u>

DATA TO BE COLLECTED: **A checklist of critical features for each intervention in the FBA-BIP will be developed and the school social worker will check with each implementer to determine if features are being implemented consistently.**

	FIDELITY EVALUATION RESULTS			
	DATE: **4/7/11**	DATE:	DATE:	DATE:
FIDELITY LEVEL (high, medium, low)	**Medium**			
ACTION TO BE TAKEN	**Arleen will problem solve with Hector about how to ensure supervision during group work**			

<u>MEASURABLE OUTCOMES</u>

PERSON RESPONSIBLE FOR EVALUATION   <u>**Andrew**</u>

DATA TO BE COLLECTED: **Daily teacher direct behavior ratings (DBRs) for inappropriate verbal behavior and physical aggression.**

SHORT TERM GOAL: **50% reduction in inappropriate verbal behavior and physical aggression from baseline by 4-1-2011.**

LONG TERM GOAL: **75% reduction in inappropriate verbal behavior and physical aggression from baseline by 11-1-2011.**

FIGURE 8.28 Continued.

LINE GRAPH OF BEHAVIOR OUTCOMES

BEHAVIOR MEASURED: __Inappropriate verbal behavior and physical aggression__

MEASUREMENT SYSTEM: __Weekly average of daily DBRs__
(e.g., DBR, SDO)

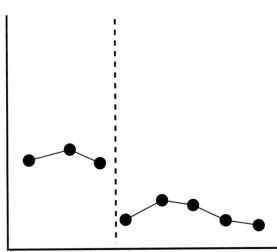

BEHAVIOR
LEVEL
(Fill in)

	Date: 3/9	Date: 3/16	Date: 3/23	Date: 3/30	Date: 4/7	Date: 4/14	Date: 4/21	Date: 4/28	Date:	Date:
BASELINE OR INTERVENTION	BL INT	BL INT	BL INT	BL INT	BL INT	BL INT	BL INT	BL INT	BL INT	BL INT

FIGURE 8.28 Continued.

ACTION	DATE WRITTEN	MEASURABLE GOAL	DATE OF REVIEW	GOAL MET? (CIRCLE)	
Arleen will problem solve with Hector about how to ensure supervision during group work	4/7/11	Group supervision will occur during 100% of Samuel's group activities		YES	NO
				YES	NO
				YES	NO
				YES	NO
				YES	NO
				YES	NO
				YES	NO

FIGURE 8.28 Continued.

Final Thoughts

The purpose of this book has been to help school social workers support the behavior of all students in a school using an expanded model of FBA based on three tiers of prevention. The specific recommendations made in this book have been offered because they conform to the literature on FBAs and have the potential to create uniformity across those implementing FBAs. The forms and details of this book, however, should be considered reasonable options but not the only options for conducting FBAs. Any procedures that provide efficient and valid information about the setting events, antecedents, and consequences of problem behavior and which can be translated into effective interventions should be considered appropriate to the support of student behavior. It is always important to remember that FBA is not a specific set of procedures, but is rather a general process of identifying the environmental conditions that predict and maintain problem behavior and inform effective interventions.

References

Albin, R. W., Lucyshyn, J. M., Horner, R. H., & Flannery, K. B. (1996). Contextual fit for behavioral support plan: A model for "goodness of fit." In L. K. Koegel, R. L. Koegel, & G. Dunlap, (Eds.), *Positive behavioral support: Including people with difficult behavior in the community* (pp. 81–98). Baltimore, MD: Paul H Brookes Publishing.

Anderson, C. A., & Scott, T. M. (2009). Implementing function based support within school-wide positive behavior support. In W. Sailor, G. Dunlap, G. Sugai, & R. H. Horner (Eds.), *Handbook of positive behavior support: Special issues in clinical child psychology* (pp. 705–28). New York: Springer.

Anderson-Butcher, D., Stetler, E., & Midle, T. (2006). A Case for Expanded School-Community Partnerships in Support of Positive Youth Development. *Children & Schools, 28,* 155–163.

Batsche, G., Elliott, J., Graden, J. L., Grimes, J., Kovelski, J. F., Prasse, D., et al. (2005). *Response to intervention: Policy considerations and implementation.* Alexandria, VA: National Association of State Directors of Special Education.

Benazzi, L., Horner, R., & Good, R. H. (2006). Effects of behavior support team composition on the technical adequacy and contextual fit of behavior support plans. *Journal of Special Education, 40,* 160–170.

Bijou, S., Peterson, R.F., & Ault, M.H. (1968). A method to integrate descriptive and experimental field studies at the level of data and empirical concepts. *Journal of Applied Behavior Analysis, 1,* 175–191.

Borgmeier, C. J. (2003). *An evaluation of informant confidence ratings as a predictive measure of the accuracy of hypotheses from functional assessment interviews.* (Doctoral dissertation). Retrieved from ProQuest Information and Learning Company (UMI No. 3095236).

Campbell, A., & Anderson, C. (2008). Enhancing effects of check-in/check-out with function based support. *Behavioral Disorders, 33,* 233–245.

Carr, E. G. (1977). The motivation of self-injurious behavior: A review of some hypotheses. *Psychological Bulletin, 84,* 800–816.

Carr, E. G., & Blakeley-Smith, A. (2006). Classroom intervention for illness-related problem behavior in children with developmental disabilities. *Behavior Modification, 30*(6), 901–924. doi: 10.1177/0145445506290080.

Chandler, L. K., & Dahlquist, C. M. (2010). *Functional assessment: Strategies to prevent and remediate challenging behavior in school settings* (3rd ed.). Upper Saddle River, NJ: Pearson Education Inc.

Chafouleas, S. M., Riley-Tillman, T. C., & Christ, T. J. (2009). Direct Behavior Rating (DBR): An emerging method for assessing social behavior within a tiered intervention system. *Assessment for Effective Intervention, 34,* 195–200. doi:10.1177/1534508409340391.

Chafouleas, S. M., Riley-Tillman, T. C., & Christ, T. J. (2010). *DBR Standard Form-Fill-in Behaviors* (Version 1.3). Retrieved from http://www.directbehaviorratings.com

Chafouleas, S. M., Riley-Tillman, T. C., Christ, T. J., & Sugai, G. (2009). *DBR Standard Form* (Version 1.4). Retrieved from http://www.directbehaviorratings.com

Christ, T. J., Riley-Tillman, C., & Chafouleas, S. M. (2009). Foundation for the development and use of direct behavior rating (DBR) to assess and evaluate student behavior. *Assessment for Effective Intervention, 34*, 201–213. doi: 10.1177/1534508409340390.

Clark, J. P., & Alvarez, M. E. (2010). Response to intervention: A call to action. In J. P. Clark & M. E. Alvarez (Eds.), *Response to intervention: A guide for school social workers*. New York: Oxford University Press.

Clark, J. P., Alvarez, M. E., Marckmann, W., & Timm, A. (2010). Supporting the adoption, implementation, and sustainability of response to intervention. In Clark, J. P., & Alvarez, M. E. (2010). *Response to intervention: A guide for school social workers*. New York: Oxford University Press.

Clark, J. P., & Gilmore, J. (2010). Tier 3 intensive individualized interventions. In J. P. Clark & M. E. Alvarez (Eds.). *Response to intervention: A guide for school social workers*. New York: Oxford University Press.

Clark, J. P., & Thiede, C. (2007). School social work practice with students with disabilities. In L. Bye & M. E. Alvarez (Eds.). *School social work theory to practice*. Belmont, CA: Thomson Brooks Cole.

Colvin, G., Kameenui, E. J., & Sugai, G. (1993). Reconceptualizing behavior management and school-wide discipline in general education. *Education and Treatment of Children, 16*(4), 361–382.

Colvin, G. Sugai, G. Good, R. H., & Lee, Y. (1997). Using active supervision and precorrection to improve transition behaviors in an elementary school. *School Psychology Quarterly, 12*, 344–363.

Cooper, J. O., Heron, T. E., & Heward, W. L. (2007). *Applied Behavior Analysis (Second Edition)*. Upper Saddle River, NJ: Pearson Education Inc.

Cormier, E. (2009). Parent involvement in functional assessment of problem behaviors related to ADHD as a basis for intervention selection. *Southern Online Journal of Nursing Research, 9*(4), 1–25. Retrieved from http://snrs.org/publications/SOJNR_articles2/Vol09Num04Art05.html

Crone, D. A., & Horner, R. H. (2003). *Building positive behavior support systems in schools: Functional behavioral assessment*. New York: The Guilford Press.

Crone, D. A., Horner, R. H., & Hawken, L. S. (2004). *Responding to problem behavior in schools: The Behavior Education Program*. New York: The Guilford Press.

Dixon, M. R., Jackson, J. W., Small, S. L., Horner-King, M. J., Mui Ker Lik, N., Garcia, Y., & Rosales, R. (2009). Creating single-subject design graphs in microsoft excel™ 2007. *Journal of Applied Behavior Analysis, 42*(2), 277–293.

Drasgow, E., Yell, M. L., Bradley, R., & Shriner, J. G. (1999). The IDEA amendments of 1997: A school-wide model for conducting functional behavioral assessments and developing behavior intervention plans. *Education and Treatment of Children, 22*(3), 244–266.

Elliott, S. N., & Gresham, F. M. (2008). *Social Skills Improvement System Intervention Guide manual*. Minneapolis, MN: Pearson Assessments.

Ervin, R. A., Radford, P. M., Bertsch, K., Piper, A. L., Ehrhardt, K. E., & Poling, A. (2001). A descriptive analysis and critique of the empirical literature on school-based functional assessment. *School Psychology Review, 30*(2), 193–210.

Fairbanks, S., Sugai, G., Guardino, D., & Lathrop, M. (2007). Response to intervention: Examining classroom behavior support in second grade. *Exceptional Children, 73*(3), 288–310.

Filter, K. J. (2004) *The functional relationship between academic variables and problem behavior: A model for assessment and intervention in the classroom* (Doctoral dissertation). University of Oregon, Eugene.

Filter, K. J., & Horner, R. H. (2009). Function-based academic interventions for problem behavior. *Education and Treatment of Children, 32*(1), 1–19.

Floyd, R. G., Phaneuf, R. L., & Wilczynski, S. M. (2005). Measurement properties of indirect assessment methods for functional behavioral assessment: A review of research. *School Psychology Review, 34*(1), 58–73.

Fynaardt, A. B, & Richardson, J. (2010). Tier 2 targeted group interventions. In J. P. Clark & M. E. Alvarez (Eds.). *Response to intervention: A guide for school social workers.* New York: Oxford University Press.

Fuchs, L. S. (2002). Best practices in defining student goals and outcomes. *Best Practices in School Psychology, 4*, 553–563.

Fuchs, D., Fuchs, L. S., & Deno, S. L. (1985). Performance instability: An identifying characteristic of learning disabled children? *Learning Disability Quarterly, 8*, 19–26.

Gresham, F. M., & Witt, J. C. (1997). Utility of intelligence tests for treatment planning, classification, and placement decisions: Recent empirical findings and future directions. *School Psychology Quarterly, 12*(3), 249–267.

Hanley, G. P., Iwata, B. A., & McCord, B. E. (2003). Functional analysis of problem behavior: A review. *Journal of Applied Behavior Analysis, 36*(2), 147–185.

Harrison, K., & Harrison, R. (2009). The school social worker's role in the tertiary support of functional assessment. *Children & Schools, 31*, 119–127.

Hartmann, D. P. (1977). Considerations in the choice of interobserver reliability estimates. *Journal of Applied Behavior Analysis, 10*(1), 103–116.

Hirsch, E. J., Lewis-Palmer, T., Sugai, G., & Schnacker, L. (2004). Using school bus discipline referral data in decision making: Two case studies. *Preventing School Failure, 48*(4), 4–9.

Horner, Carr, Halle, McGee, Odom, Wolery. (2005). The use of single-subject research to identify evidence-based practice in special education. *Exceptional Children, 71*(2), 165–179.

Horner, R. H., Day, H. M., & Day, J. R. (1997). Using neutralizing routines to reduce problem behaviors. *Journal of Applied Behavior Analysis, 30*(4), 601–614.

Horner, R. H., Sugai, G., Todd, A. W., & Lewis-Palmer, T. (2005). School-wide positive behavior support: An alternative approach to discipline in schools. In L. Bambara & L. Kern (Eds.), *Individualized supports for students with problem behaviors: Designing positive behavior plans.* New York: The Guilford Press.

Illinois PBIS Network. (2010). PBIS Glossary of Abbreviations and Terms. Retrieved September 25, 2010 from http://community.pbisillinois.org/Home/pbis-glossary

---

Ingram, K., Lewis-Palmer, T., & Sugai, G. (2005). Function-based intervention planning: Comparing the effectiveness of FBA function-based and non-function-based intervention plans. *Journal of Positive Behavior Interventions* 7(4), 224–236.

Irvin, L. K., Tobin, T. J., Sprague, J. R., Sugai, G., & Vincent, C. G. (2004). Validity of office discipline referral measures as indices of school-wide behavioral status and effects of school-wide behavioral interventions. *Journal of Positive Behavior Interventions,* 6(3), 131–147.

Iwata B. A., Dorsey M. F., Slifer, K. J., Bauman K. E., & Richman G. S. (1982). Toward a functional analysis of self-injury. *Analysis and Intervention in Developmental Disabilities, 2,* 3–20.

Johnston, J. M., & Pennypacker, H. S. (1993). *Strategies and tactics of behavioral research* (2nd ed.). Hillsdale, NJ: Lawrence Erlbaum Associates.

Jozefowics-Simbeni, D. (2008). An ecological and developmental perspective on dropout risk factors in early adolescence: Role of school social workers in dropout prevention efforts. *Children & Schools, 30,* 49–62.

Kennedy, C. H., & Itkonen, T. (1993). Effects of setting events on the problem behavior of students with severe disabilities. *Journal of Applied Behavior Analysis, 26*(3), 321–327.

Kern, L., & Clemens, N. H. (2007). Antecedent strategies to promote appropriate classroom behavior. *Psychology in the Schools, 44*(1), 65–75. doi: 10.1002/pits.20206.

Kern, L., Gallagher, P., Starosta, K., Hickman, W., & George, M. (2006). Longitudinal outcomes of functional assessment-based interventions. *Journal of Positive Behavior Interventions, 8,* 67–78.

Lane, K. L., Weisenbach, J. L., Little, M. A., Phillips, A., & Wehby, J. (2006). Illustrations of function-based interventions implemented by general education teachers: Building capacity at the school site. *Education and Treatment of Children, 29,* 549–571.

Luiselli, J. K., Putnam, R. F., & Sunderland, M. (2002). Longitudinal evaluation of behavior support intervention in a public middle school. *Journal of Positive Behavior Interventions, 4*(3), 182–188.

Maag, J. W., & Larson, P. J. (2004). Training a general education teacher to apply functional assessment. *Education and Treatment of Children, 27,* 26–36.

Mace, C. F., & Roberts, M. L. (1993). Developing effective interventions. Empirical and conceptual considerations. In J. Reichle & D.P. Wacker (Eds.). *Communicative alternatives to challenging behavior: Integrating functional assessment and intervention strategies.* Baltimore, MD: Paul H. Brookes.

March, R. E., & Horner, R. H. (2002). Feasibility and contributions of functional behavioral assessment in schools. *Journal of Emotional and Behavioral Disorders, 10,* 158–170.

March, R. E., Horner, R. H., Lewis-Palmer, T., Brown, D., Crone, D., Todd, A.W., & Carr, E. (2000). *Functional Assessment Checklist for Teachers and Staff.* Eugene, OR: Educational and Community Supports.

May, S., Ard, W., III., Todd, A. W., Horner, R. H., Sugai, G., Glasgow, A., & Sprague, J. R. (2010). School-wide information system. Retrieved from http://www.swis.org

McIntosh, K., Borgmeier, C., Anderson, C. M., Horner, R. H., Rodriguez, B. J., & Tobin, T. J. (2008). Technical adequacy of the functional assessment checklist: Teachers and staff

(FACTS) FBA interview measure. *Journal of Positive Behavior Interventions, 10,* 33–45. doi: 10.1177/1098300707311619.

McIntosh, K., Brown, J. A., & Borgmeier, C. J. (2008). Validity of functional behavior assessment within a response to intervention framework: Evidence, recommended practice, and future directions. *Assessment for Effective Intervention, 34*(1), 6–14. doi: 10.1177/1534508408314096.

McIntosh, K., Campbell, A. L., Carter, D. R., & Dickey, C. R. (2009). Differential effects of a tier two behavior intervention based on function of problem behavior. *Journal of Positive Behavior Intervention, 11*(2), 82–93.

McIntosh, K., Frank, J. L., & Spaulding, S. A. (2010). Establishing research-based trajectories of office discipline referrals for individual students. *School Psychology Review, 39*(3), 380–394.

McNeill, S. L., Watson, T. S., Henington, C., & Meeks, C. (2002). The effects of training parents in functional behavior assessment on problem identification, problem analysis, and intervention design. *Behavior Modification, 26*(4), 499–515.

Medley, N. S., Little, S. G., & Akin-Little, A. (2008). Comparing individual behavior plans from schools with and without schoolwide positive behavior support: A preliminary study. *Journal of Behavioral Education, 17,* 93–110. doi: 10.1007/s10864-007-9053-y.

Michael, J. (1974). Statistical inference for individual organism research: mixed blessing or curse. *Journal of Applied Behavior Analysis, 7*(4), 647–653.

Miltenberger, R. G. (2004). *Behavior modification: Principles and procedures* (3rd ed.). Belmont, CA: Wadsworth.

Munk, D. D., & Repp, A. C. (1994). Behavioral assessment of feeding problems of individuals with severe disabilities. *Journal of Applied Behavior Analysis, 27,* 241–250.

National Association of Social Workers Code of Ethics. (2008). *NASW Code of Ethics.* Retrieved July 1, 2010 at http://www.socialworkers.org/pubs/code/code.asp

Nelson, J. R., & Carr, B. A. (1996). *The think time strategy for schools: Bringing order to the classroom.* Longmont, CO: Sopris West.

Newcomer, L. L., & Lewis, T. J. (2004). Functional behavioral assessment: An investigation of assessment reliability and effectiveness of function-based interventions. *Journal of Emotional and Behavioral Disorders, 12*(3), 168–181.

O'Neill, R. E., Horner, R. H., Albin, R. W., Sprague, J. R., Storey, K., & Newton, J. S. (1997). *Functional assessment and program development for problem behavior: A practical handbook* (2nd ed.). Pacific Grove, CA: Brooks Cole Publishing.

Office of Special Education Programs (OSEP) Center on Positive Behavioral Interventions and Supports. (2004). *Implementation blueprint and self-assessment school-wide positive behavioral interventions and supports.* Retrieved July 30, 2010 from http://www.pbis.org/common/pbisresources/publications/SWPBS_Implementation_Blueprint_v_May_9_2010.pdf

Patterson, S. T. (2009). The effects of teacher- student small talk on out-of-seat behavior. *Education and Treatment of Children, 32,* 167–174.

Pelios, L., Morren, J., Tesch, D., & Axelrod, S. (1999). The impact of functional analysis methodology on treatment choice for self-injurious and aggressive behavior. *Journal of Applied Behavior Analysis, 32*(2), 185–195.

Reschly, D. J., & Tilly, W. D. (1999). Reform trends and system design alternatives. In D. J. Reschly, W. D. Tilly, & J. P. Grimes (Eds.), *Special education in transition: Functional assessment and noncategorical programming* (pp. 19–48). Longmont, CO: Sopris West.

Reynolds, C. R., & Kamphaus, R. W. (2004). *Behavior assessment system for children* (2nd ed.). Pearson Assessments.

Riley-Tillman, T. C., Christ, T. J., Chafouleas, S. M., Boice, C. H., & Briesch, A. (2010). The impact of observation duration on the accuracy of data obtained from direct behavior rating (DBR). *Journal of Positive Behavior Interventions*, 1–10. doi: 10.1177/1098300710361954.

Riley-Tillman, T. C., Chafouleas, S. M., Sassu, K. A., Chanese, J. A. M., & Glazer, A. D. (2008). Examining the agreement of direct behavior ratings and systematic direct observation data for on-task and disruptive behavior. *Journal of Positive Behavior Interventions*, *10*(2), 136–143.

Ross, L. (1977). The intuitive psychologist and his shortcomings: Distortions in the attribution process. In L. Berkowitz (Ed.), *Advances in experimental social psychology* (vol. 10). New York: Academic Press.

Ross S. W., & Horner, R. H. (2009). Bully prevention in positive behavior support. *Journal of Applied Behavior Analysis*, *42*(4), 747–759.

Salend, S. J., & Taylor, L. S. (2002). Cultural perspectives: Missing pieces in the functional assessment process. *Intervention in School and Clinic*, *38*(2), 104–112.

Salvia, J., & Ysseldyke, J. E. (2001). *Assessment* (8th ed.). Boston, MA: Houghton Mifflin Company.

Saudargas, R. A., & Zanolli, K. (1990). Momentary time sampling as an estimate of percentage time: A field validation. *Journal of Applied Behavior Analysis*, *23*(4), 533–537.

Schlientz, M. D., Riley-Tillman, T. C., Briesch, A. M., Walcott, C. M., & Chafouleas, S. M., (2009) The impact of training on the accuracy of Direct Behavior Ratings (DBRs). *School Psychology Quarterly*, *24*, 73–83. doi:10.1037/a0016255.

Scott, T. M., & Eber, L. (2003). Functional assessment and wraparound as systemic school processes: Primary, secondary, and tertiary systems examples. *Journal of Positive Behavior Interventions*, *5*(3), 131–143.

Scott, T. M., Liaupsin, C., Nelson, C. M., & McIntyre. (2005). Team-based functional behavior assessments as a proactive public school process: A descriptive analysis of current barriers. *Journal of Behavioral Education*, *14*(1), 57–71.

Scott, T. M., McIntyre, J., Liaupsin, C., Nelson, C. M., Conroy, M., & Payne, L. D. (2005). An examination of the relation between functional behavior assessment and selected intervention strategies with school-based teams. *Journal of Positive Behavior Interventions*, *7*, 205–215.

Shaffer, G. L. (2007). History of school social work. In L. Bye & M. Alvarez (Eds.). *School social work theory to practice*. Belmont, CA: Thomson Brooks Cole.

Shinn, M. R. (1986). Does anyone care what happens after the refer-test-place sequence: The systematic evaluation of special education program effectiveness. *School Psychology Review*, *15*(1), 49-58.

Skiba, R., & Peterson, R., (1999). The dark side of zero tolerance: Can punishment lead to safe schools? *Phi Delta Kappan, 80*(5), 372–382.

Skiba, R. J., Peterson, R. L., & Williams, T. (1997). Office referrals and suspension: Disciplinary intervention in middle schools. *Education and Treatment of Children, 20*(3), 295–315.

Skinner, B. F. (1938). *The behavior of organisms: An experimental analysis.* New York: Appleton-Century-Crofts.

Skinner, B. F. (1953). *Science and human behavior.* New York: Macmillan.

Skinner, C. H., Neddenriep, C. E., Robinson, S. L., Ervin, R., & Jones, K. (2002). Altering educational environments through positive peer reporting: Prevention and remediation of social problems associated with behavior disorders. *Psychology in the School, 39,* 191–202.

Spaulding, S. A., Irvin, L. K., Horner, R. H., May, S. L., Emeldi, M., Tobin, T. J., & Sugai, G. (2010). Schoolwide social-behavioral climate, student problem behavior, and related administrative decisions: Empirical patterns from 1,510 schools nationwide. *Journal of Positive Behavior Interventions, 12*(2), 69–85.

Sprague, J., & Golly, A. (2005). *Best behavior: Building positive behavior support in schools.* Boston, MA: Sopris West.

Sprague, J., & Horner, R. H. (2006). Schoolwide positive behavior supports. In S. Jimerson, & M. Furlong (Eds.), *Handbook of school violence and school safety: From research to practice* (pp. 413–27). Hillsdale, NJ: Lawrence Erlbaum Associates.

Stahr, B., Cushing, D., Lane, K., & Fox, J. (2006). Efficacy of a function-based intervention in decreasing off-task behavior exhibited by a student with ADHD. *Journal of Positive Behavior Interventions, 8,* 201–212. doi:10.1177/10983007060080040301.

Steege, M. W., & Watson, T. S. (2009). *Conducting school-based functional behavior assessment: A practitioner's guide (second edition).* New York: The Guilford Press.

Sugai, G., & Horner, R. H. (2002). The evolution of discipline practices: School-wide positive behavior supports. *Child and Family Behavior Therapy, 24*(1–2), 23–50.

Sugai, G., Lewis-Palmer, T., & Hagan, S. (1998). Using functional assessments to develop behavior support plans. *Preventing School Failure, 43*(1), 71–78.

Thorndike, E. L. (1913). *Educational psychology: The psychology of learning.* New York: Teachers College Press.

Todd, A. W., Campbell, A. L., Meyer, G. G., & Horner, R. H. (2008). The effects of a targeted intervention to reduce problem behaviors. *Journal of Positive Behavior Interventions, 10,* 46–55.

Tracy, E., & Usaj, K. (2007). School social work with individuals and small groups. In L. Bye & M. E. Alvarez (Eds.). *School Social Work Theory to Practice.* Belmont, CA: Thomson Brooks Cole.

Tucker, M., Sigafoos, J., & Bushell, H. (1998). Use of noncontingent reinforcement in the treatment of challenging behavior: A review and clinical guide. *Behavior Modification, 22,* 529–47. doi: 10.1177/01454455980224005.

Umbreit, J., Lane, K. L., & Dejud, C. (2004). Improving classroom behavior by modifying task difficulty: Effects of increasing the difficulty of too-easy tasks. *Journal of Positive Behavioral Interventions, 6*(1), 13–20.

Vollmer, T. R., & Borrero, C. S. W. (2009). Noncontingent reinforcement as a treatment for problem behavior. In W. T. O'Donohue, & J. E. Fisher (Eds.), *General principles and empirically supported techniques of cognitive behavior therapy*, (pp. 465–472). Hoboken, NJ: John Wiley & Sons Inc.

Von Ravensberg, H., & Tobin, T. J. (2006). *IDEA 2004: Final Regulations and the Reauthorized Functional Behavioral Assessment*. Eugene, OR: University of Oregon, College of Education, Educational and Community Supports.

Walker, H. L., Horner, R. H., Sugai, G., Bullis, M., Sprague, J. R., Bricker, D., & Kaufman, M. J. (1996). Integrated approaches to preventing antisocial behavior patterns among school-age children and youth. *Journal of Emotional and Behavioral Disorders*, 4(4), 194–209.

Watson, J. B. (1924). *Behaviorism*. New York: Norton.

Watson, T. S., & Wickstrom, K. (2004). *Review of the Behavior Assessment System for Children* (2nd ed.). *Mental Measurement Yearbook*. Lincoln, NE: Buros Institute of Mental Measurements.

Westling, D. (2010). Teachers and challenging behavior: Knowledge, views, and practices. *Remedial and Special Education*, 31(1), 48–63.

Index

Forms developed for this book by the authors are available for free download and use at the following websites: http://www.mnsu.edu/psych/psyd/people/ filter/ and http://www.mnsu.edu/psych/people/kevin_f.html